MW00529009

con·text \ˈkän-ˌtekst\ *noun*
1 : the parts of a discourse that surround a word or passage and can throw light on its meaning 2 : the interrelated conditions in which something exists or occurs :

Changed

COMPELLING SCRIPTURES THAT
CHANGED A PRE-TRIBULATION
RAPTURE BELIEVER FOREVER

WILL *YOU* BE CHANGED?

Steven Straub

New
Bereans
Press

New
Bereans
Press

Changed©
Copyright 2011 by Steven Straub

Requests for information can be addressed to:

Steven Straub
414 Hudson Hill Rd.
Hudson, Maine 04449
USA

Email: skydiver@midmaine.com
Website: www.theposttribulationrapture.com

All Scripture quotations are taken from the Authorized King James Version—a copyright-free publication.

All rights reserved. No part of this publication may be reproduced, stored in a retrieval system, or transmitted in any form or by any means—electronic, mechanical, photocopy, recording, or any other—except for brief quotations in printed reviews, without the prior permission of the author.

Cover photo (prior to alteration) by John Dalkin
Cover design and interior diagrams by Steven Straub

Printed in the United States of America.

First Paperback Edition

Dedicated to my Lord and personal Savior Jesus Christ who has graciously showered me with wisdom, insight, inspiration, guidance, and patience to write every word within. Without Him, I would be nothing, and this work would have never come to fruition.

Also to:

the reader who will be changed.

Acknowledgments

I would like to thank Doug and Andrew Smith for taking time out of their busy schedules to help edit this manuscript; it was greatly appreciated!

Also, a special thanks to Biblegateway.com and Biblos.com for their fabulous websites. They offer a quick and easy way to search the Scriptures and made my innumerable hours of research much less complicated.

Finally, I would like to thank my Parents who are both astute studiers of the Word and who have both remained faithful to the Lord throughout my years. Being raised in a Christ-centered home has had a profound impact on me and ultimately, without your Godly examples, my passion for prophecy would have remained dormant, and this book would have never come into existence.

But if the watchman see the sword come, and blow not the trumpet, and the people be not warned; if the sword come, and take any person from among them, he is taken away in his iniquity; but his blood will I require at the watchman's hand.

Ezekiel 33:6

Contents

Author's Foreword

The rapture. If you're a believer, this word fills you with an immediate sense of hope and joy. To think that, someday, Jesus Christ is physically coming back to gather together His church is very exciting indeed. That's the good news. The bad news is the sad reality of utter confusion surrounding this event that has ultimately infiltrated and fractured the church into a variety of subgroups—confusion that even capitalizes on the very word "rapture." For this reason, I would like to state that I am not a proponent of the word "rapture"—not because it's nowhere to be found in the English translation of Scripture, but for one other simple reason. Although most consider the word to be insignificant, I believe it fosters the tiny spark needed to fuel the fire of a broader deception— mainly that of its timing. It has become a trigger word that has so many Christians brainwashed into quickly associating it with a skillfully devised position whether they consciously realize it or not. Although I agree that it can legitimately be interpreted as "caught up," and unarguably is to involve those who are alive in Christ at His coming, the connotations and controversy that surround it these days are quite deceiving as the Word will hopefully soon reveal to you. As a result, when I use the word "rapture" in this book, it will be italicized to emphasize its double nature.

Brothers and sisters, it's time to get back to the Word of God and stop conforming to the words of men. I'm not just throwing you a tired old cliché; I really emphasize it because it's important. If you allow man to interpret Scripture for you without ever checking into it for yourself, you are eventually going to find yourself in a whole lot of trouble doctrinally down the road—it's only a matter of time.

My pastor encourages us to take notes during his messages. Why? Because he states emphatically: "Just because I said it, it doesn't make it right!" How true that is! We can't just take his word for it! We must take the *Word's* word for it! We must hold man's doctrine accountable at *all* times. Does it submit or conflict with the Bible? If it conflicts, then we must return and submit to the Word quickly and without a biased mindset. In the end, God's Word is final authority.

Preface

My question was not whether the *rapture* would occur. I've always known deep down that this event will someday become a reality, but it was more a question of when! Unfortunately, there were many theories floating around the church that eventually had me scratching my head in confusion. Some were saying this, others were teaching that, and all the while I felt like something was missing. I wanted truth.

I was raised the son of a Baptist preacher and missionary and was absolutely saturated with the Word of God for as long as I can remember. If anyone had a well-grounded Christian upbringing, it was certainly me! I made a profession of faith almost as soon as I could understand the concept. In my teenage years, I strayed from the Lord, but even in those times of distancing, I occasionally found myself flipping through various parts of Scripture. Even then, I noticed a thirst for prophecy beginning to develop.

I grew up with the teaching that the *rapture* could occur at any moment but that this moment would most definitely occur before the last "seven years of tribulation" that would come upon the earth prior to Christ's physical return in glory. This teaching is recognized as the pre-tribulation *rapture* theory. Later, I would learn of a mid-tribulation theory which places the *rapture* three and a half years prior to Christ's actual return. In recent years, a viewpoint known as the pre-wrath position has established itself and is essentially a close relative to the post-tribulation view. Of course, there are a few variations of these major end time positions, but I will save you the headache.

I settled on the pre-tribulation *rapture* theory as truth and believed what everyone else believed. The *rapture* of the church takes place, a wake of chaos ensues, the Antichrist rises to power, the tribulation saints endure severe persecution, and afterward, us *raptured* folk return from heaven, with Christ, to wage war against Satan and his minions at the battle of Armageddon. It definitely sounded appealing; why shouldn't I trust them? After all, they were good-standing, Bible-believing, God-fearing, Spirit-filled Christians. They couldn't possibly have it wrong—right? Besides, it seemed that every single one of them believed it, so it had to be true! Even preachers on the other side of the country were preaching it on television and radio! How could they all be wrong? The problem began, however, when I started reading passages regarding the *rapture* for myself. Immediately, I encountered blaring discrepancies that I had to overlook in order for me to believe what everyone else believed. Was there something wrong with my interpretation or was it everyone else?

When I finally came back to the Lord, I began seeking God daily for general wisdom through prayer and fasting. It was on one particular sunny day, sitting in my chair, that I was reading Scripture regarding the return of Christ, when I was literally *raptured* into the truth! I experienced, what seemed like, an instant download from above and from then on, I was forever *changed!* This download continued throughout the following months, further cementing my original transformation. He knew my desire in this area was a deep-seeded one (which I believe He placed in me) and had begun watering it so I could grow in knowledge.

I must intervene quickly here so as to be perfectly honest with you and admit that I'm not what most would consider a Bible scholar. I didn't attend a Bible College. I don't have a PHD; I wasn't formally trained in anyway. I'd only wear a tie if my life was threatened, and I don't wear suits. I'm a horrible public speaker; a man of few words (outspoken words anyway!). I don't like to stand out in a crowd, and just thinking about it makes me instantly sweat. If you think any of that cramps my credibility, then get in line behind me because I've already pleaded my case before God that He has the wrong guy for this job! Somehow, I don't think He's listening. I'm just an average guy carrying around a King James Version of the Bible with a not-so-average thirst for the truth.

The only justification I can find is that I am all of those things. Just a short flip through the Bible reveals countless examples of "write-offs" that God used to bring about His purposes. Perhaps in using this "write-off," He's making a point that any average Joe can wade through countless opinions of reputable men yet still come to the truth on their own. I'm not the dullest knife in the draw but trust me; if I can do it, you can do it.

Now I'm not a wolf in sheep's clothing come to steal the "blessed hope." I don't get my jollies from being confrontational. I'm not out to make a buck by coming up with wild spin-off ideas, and I'm not into scare tactics. *I yearn for truth and nothing else.* Believe me, it's not like I was looking for any avenue to proclaim persecution in my quest to find answers. In fact, it would be my last choice if I had one. Really, I would enjoy nothing more than to be *raptured* off this planet before severe persecution came my way—sign me up and show me the front of the line could ya?! Unfortunately, the problem I have found in my many hours of intense studying is that the Bible teaches us something entirely different.

I know that some of you are already rolling your eyes: "Here we go again; another screwball pushing doom and gloom, trying to cause division amongst the people." I assure you, this is not my intention. In fact, it is quite the opposite. I am all about unification— it makes us stronger as a body, but that unification must be under the banner of *truth*. I will accept no other form. Anything other than truth is, quite frankly, deceit.

I ask that you at least read this book in its entirety. Read it from one hand, and have your Bible open in the other. You should check out *everything* I am proposing. I *want* you to do it. Additionally, make every possible attempt to set aside pre-conceived ideas that might make you quickly disregard what is confronting you. Once you have done all of that, *then* weigh the evidence and make up your *own* mind. If at that point, you're still rolling your eyes, then go ahead; use this book to prop up that old couch. However, my prayer is that, by the last page, your eyes won't be rolling from one side to the other, but instead will be looking up to the Father for a renewed preparedness of what's to come.

May God enrich you always with wisdom, guidance and a meek and prepared heart to receive all that is yours from the Father this day. In the Name of our Lord Jesus Christ I pray. Amen.

Introduction

It has been my intent from the very beginning of this work to present a clear case for the post-tribulation *rapture* of the church from a very simple and logical approach—characteristics that are representative of the position itself. Unlike other viewpoints, it's actually one of the easiest to grasp because it adheres to the most literal and logical of interpretations. In fact, to understand it fully takes one unusual yet critical element: <u>*Simplicity*</u>. You're actually going to have to simplify your thinking! I know that sounds odd, but people are under the impression these days that it's impossible for them to understand prophecy without buying a 50lb book to explain it all to them bit by bit. There's been such a bombardment of well-crafted theories and opinions spewing out 1000 page exegeses on each tiny aspect of the Second Coming, it's no wonder people think they need a Bible-genius-guide just to sort it all out for them first! I've come here to tell you that it doesn't have to be this way. What needs to be readdressed is that you can, in fact, understand Bible prophecy *for yourself*. People need to be reminded of that in this day and age. Every time *you* pick up the Word of God, *you* hold the key to unlocking the truth. All that's needed is a straightforward and literal approach. I'm not trying to make light of Bible scholars; they certainly are an asset to the church (when they are in the truth), but God has also designed His Word for the layman among us—not just for the PHD. He wants *all* to come into His truth.

When Google, the now-famous internet search engine worth multiple billions, was still in its infancy, they began running tests on their home page and collecting users' opinions. What they observed was a peculiar similarity in behavior amongst the majority of their subjects. They found that eighty to ninety percent of users waited up to thirty seconds before typing in a search query. When asked why they waited so long, the answer was the same every time: They were waiting for the rest of the page to load! You see, Google's objective from the very beginning was to provide a simple search solution. However, people, at that time, were so used to a bombardment of links, banners, "pop-ups," and advertisements on their search engine pages, they didn't even realize it was completely unnecessary to begin with, and what they truly needed had already been right in front of them all along! The same principle can be applied to the study of prophecy. If recognized, the Bible offers its users simplicity. However, there are those who tend to *"over-scholarize"* (over-scholar-eyes) what is already a very simple and established truth and are too busy searching for "pop-ups" that were never really there to begin with. Unfortunately, in the end, they miss out on the answer sitting right in front of them.

Have you ever had somebody ask you to help them look for their glasses and immediately you realized that they were actually sitting on top of the poor person's head? They had been frantically searching for them, ripping apart every nook and cranny, and they didn't realize how easy the solution really was. The answer was on them the *whole time* yet they had forgotten how simple it was to find what they were looking for. Again, this same principle can be applied to the study of prophecy. A subject can be critiqued to such a great extent that the truth is completely ignored! If it had just been left to its literal interpretation, then the only thing that would have been "left behind" was confusion. The old acronym is K.I.S.S.—*Keep it simple stupid.* There is much wisdom in this humorous adage, and it certainly applies to Bible interpretation as well.

It has also been my intention from the start to make every attempt to abstain from "theory-bashing" because I want to present the truth in love. However, since my personal testimony involves a *rapture* out of the pre-tribulation theory—translated into the post-tribulation view—then it is only logical that I point out the discrepancies that sent me out onto this new path. Please understand that in doing so, I am not trying to offend—but to *amend* the multitude of differences the church has concerning this controversial area of doctrine. While I know I'm fighting a very large and daunting uphill battle, I also know that God has good things in store for the true church in the coming days, and I believe that unity of eschatological doctrine can be one of them if we just submit our will to His. It is Biblically clear that during the coming atrocity, the saints will be well-grounded in their resolve during the great tribulation—even unto death. If those particular saints are to be identified as the church, that fact is indicative of this very unification.

While this work is essentially tailored to those of you who currently hold to the pre-tribulation *rapture* theory, I want to assure the rest that I have not forgotten about those who are either new to the faith and are looking for real answers, those who are uncertain about what they currently believe, or even those who are simply searching for more weapons to add to their "post-trib" arsenal. Keep on reading!

-*Rapture Revealed*-

Before we dive into this fascinating subject, I want to make sure that we are all well aware of the most common terms. I assume the majority of you are already somewhat familiar with the *rapture* and what it entails, but for those who aren't, let me first quickly summarize it for you so that you have a basic understanding. The first major *rapture* passage is found in the first book of Corinthians.

> *I Corinthians 15:51-53*
> *51Behold, I shew you a mystery; We shall not all sleep, but we shall all be* **changed**,
> *52In a moment, in the twinkling of an eye, at the last trump: for the trumpet shall sound, and the dead shall be raised incorruptible, and we shall be* **changed**.
> *53For this corruptible must put on incorruption, and this mortal must put on* **immortality**.

The second major passage to speak of this same unique event can be found in the first book of Thessalonians. The origin of the word *rapture* is also found here—based solely on the Latin Vulgate. It's derived from the Latin word "rapiemur" which is translated as "we shall be *raptured*" or "we shall be caught up."

> *I Thessalonians 4:16-17*
> *16For the Lord himself shall descend from heaven with a shout, with the voice of the archangel, and*

with the trump of God: and the dead in Christ shall rise first:
¹⁷Then we which are alive and remain shall be caught up *together with them in the clouds, to meet the Lord in the air: and so shall we ever be with the Lord.*

This is certainly an exciting prospect for any son or daughter of God! What an image it brings to mind when reading these passages! There will be one generation in the near future that will literally escape the grip of death! They will first witness Christ descending from heaven with a shout, followed by the dead in Christ who will rise from their graves. Then, they themselves will be transformed in a millisecond—being caught up into the air to be with the Lord forever. There is much evidence surrounding today's generation that makes it *the* prime candidate to partake in this *rapture* event, and the thought of this very real possibility is truly mind-altering if you dwell on it!

There are two parts to this amazing event. The first part is the resurrection. The resurrection will involve all true believers who have previously died before Christ's actual return. Their graves will open up, and those who have "slept" will "awaken" to everlasting life. This resurrection is a concept that originated in the Old Testament, is a word found scattered throughout the New Testament, and was even specifically mentioned by Christ numerous times during His ministry.

The second part is the "caught up" or "changed" event which has come to be known as the famous *rapture*. This will involve the true followers of Christ who are *still alive and remain* after the resurrection of the dead occurs. It will happen in the "twinkling of an eye"—occurring instantaneously! One second you're here. Before the next second hits, you'll be transformed into a glorious body, rising supernaturally to meet the Lord in the air! Again, the order is the resurrection of the dead, followed by the *rapture* of the living. Take note of this because it becomes important later.

-*The Great Tribulation*-

Since this book is specifically curtailed to the timing of the church *rapture* in relation to the great tribulation, a short description of this coming period is also needed for those of you who are unfamiliar with the term. Christ makes the first literal mention of "great tribulation" in Matthew 24 in strict association with the abomination of desolation spoken of by the prophet Daniel.

> *Matthew 24:15,21*
> *15When ye therefore shall see the abomination of desolation, spoken of by Daniel the prophet, stand in the holy place, (whoso readeth, let him understand:)*
> *21For then shall be **great tribulation**, such as was not since the beginning of the world to this time, no, nor ever shall be*

To be that reader of understanding, a look at the book of Daniel is needed to grasp what Christ was referring to.

> *Daniel 9:27*
> *And he (the Antichrist) shall confirm the covenant with many for one week: and in the midst of the week he shall cause the sacrifice and the oblation to cease, and for the overspreading of abominations he shall make it desolate, even until the consummation, and that determined shall be poured upon the desolate.*

It's well known in most circles that the "week" being spoken of here is referring to a seven year timeline. The Jews use the term "week" to describe either a week of days or a week of years. Here, the context was years. Daniel stated that the Antichrist (whom I will reveal later) will confirm the covenant with many for one seven year period. In the "midst" of this seven year covenant, the Antichrist will retract, make sacrifices unlawful, and set up an abomination to be worshipped in its place. This abomination set up by the Antichrist *in the middle* of the seven year period is what Christ specifically refers to in Matthew 24 as the *beginning* of "great tribulation."

Because the great tribulation begins its campaign in the middle of the last seven years before Christ returns, then basic math dictates it to be three and a half years in duration. Fortunately, Daniel's prophecy reiterates this very fact further along in chapter 12.

Daniel 12:11
And from the time that the daily sacrifice shall be taken away, and the abomination that maketh desolate set up, there shall be a **thousand two hundred and ninety days.**

The angel informs Daniel during his visitation that the end of all the things shown to him will come 1290 days after the Antichrist sets up the abomination of desolation, confirming that it is, indeed, three and a half years in length.

The book of Revelation is essentially a prophetic carbon copy of Daniel and explains certain aspects of Daniel's prophecies in further detail. In Revelation chapter 13, it's addressed yet again.

Revelation 13:4-5,7
*4And they worshipped the dragon which gave power
unto the beast: and they worshipped the beast, saying, Who is like unto the beast? who is able to make
war with him?*
*5And there was given unto him a mouth speaking
great things and blasphemies; and power was given
unto him to continue **forty and two months**.*
*7And it was given unto him to make war with the
saints, and to overcome them: and power was given
him over all kindreds, and tongues, and nations.*

When the Beast arises (the worldwide, end time Satanic
kingdom ruled by Antichrist), the Antichrist will summon
the source of his power from Satan for a period of 42
months. A quick calculation reveals this 42 month period to
be three and a half years in length, providing verification
yet again. It is also during this period that the saints of God
are to be overcome physically by this particular ruthless
leader, revealing the highest form of persecution the elect
must endure just prior to the Second Coming of Christ—
thus Christ's assertion on the term "great tribulation."

Clearly, Scripture is very specific in presenting an abun-
dance of information about the last half of the last week of
Daniel—directly identified by Jesus Christ as a "time of
great tribulation"—while making very little mention about
the first half. The most notable and literal mention is found
in Daniel 9:27 and even then, it's in conjunction with the
entire seven year course, and isn't set apart for scrutiny,
making it truly less than significant in relation. It is to be
noted that Scripture offers absolutely no literal correlation
between the word "tribulation" and the *first* half of Daniel's
seventieth week. Much emphasis has been given by some to
the first half in this manner, but the Bible concentrates its

effort on the last half, not only in activity, but also in duration because that will commence the actual time of great tribulation, unique since the foundation of the world, and worthy enough of specific mention by both the Messiah and the Prophets.

-The Second Coming of Christ-

Upon informing His disciples about the time of great tribulation, Christ then extends the prophetic timeline one step further to include a description of His return.

> *Matthew 24:29-30*
> *29Immediately after the tribulation of those days shall the sun be darkened, and the moon shall not give her light, and the stars shall fall from heaven, and the powers of the heavens shall be shaken:*
> *30And then shall appear the sign of the Son of man in heaven: and then shall all the tribes of the earth mourn, and they shall see the Son of man coming in the clouds of heaven with power and great glory.*

All of this information, in unison, reveals a specific order to end time events that begins with the Antichrist's covenant confirmed with many for seven years. This will be followed by the "abomination of desolation" which will be set up in the midst of this seven year period, becoming the catalyst for the segment of time known as the great tribulation. This great tribulation timeframe will continue for a period of three and one-half years. Immediately after the great tribulation, Christ will return from heaven with great power and immense glory to wage war at the battle of Armageddon and judge the world for its wickedness while the elect of God are simultaneously ushered into the blessings of God's kingdom which will have then descended from the heavens onto earth. The heartbeat of this Godly kingdom will be centered in the city of Jerusalem where Jesus Christ—King of all kings—will finally sit on His glorious throne in the line of David and rule the world with a rod of iron, fulfilling the relevant prophecies written so long ago with complete and total accuracy.

Dear Heavenly Father,

I pray that You guide me in all aspects of this writing. Help me to discern Your voice. Keep me from my own speculations and interpretations that allow deceit to seep in. Keep me in truth always by filling me with Your words. I pray for Your strength in me and not my own. Father, I also ask that You illuminate these words supernaturally to all who are appointed to receive them from You. In the Name of your Son, Jesus Christ, I pray these things. Amen.

The Day of the Lord

Now that a basic understanding of both the great tribulation period and the *rapture* has been obtained, the next question becomes an obvious one—where does the *rapture* of the church fit into the end time prophetic equation? Will it occur before, during, or after the great tribulation? Truly, this has become a black-hole question of the believers' universe! The return of Christ and the "catching away" of the church will be *the* premier event in human history but, unfortunately, this topic has succumbed to much heated debate within the church. How did it come to this? The reason there's so much controversy surrounding the *rapture* timing is *because somebody's not telling the truth.* In the end, the church *rapture* will unfold in one particular way and at one particular time, yet a vast multitude of opinions have popped up, causing in-house rivalries. However, it is of great fortune that God does, in fact, want us to be well advised on when this future *rapture* event will take place and offers many signposts on the prophetic map as a guide. Unfortunately, many are trying to discredit this very simple message by twisting, contorting, and separating key components of the Word.

The first and most destructive distortion concerns an

event referred to in Scripture as the *day of the Lord*. Let's begin with one of the two major *rapture* passages, starting in I Thessalonians.

> *I Thessalonians 4:16-17*
> *¹⁶For the Lord himself shall descend from heaven with a shout, with the voice of the archangel, and with the trump of God: and the dead in Christ shall rise first:*
> *¹⁷Then we which are alive and remain shall be **caught up** together with them in the clouds, to meet the Lord in the air: and so shall we ever be with the Lord*
> *¹⁸Wherefore comfort one another with these words.*

These few popular verses have become *the* cornerstone Scripture for pre-tribulation *rapture* theorists. They put most, if not all of their eggs into this basket. The problem is they stop reading! If they hadn't stopped, they would have come across the following verse:

> *I Thessalonians 5:1*
> *But of the times and the seasons, brethren, ye have no need that I write unto you.*

I need to stop for a brief moment and emphasize that context is extremely important when interpreting Scripture. In fact, it's one of the most essential tools to have in your toolbox if you want to get the absolute truth from a passage. It's the best way to *simplify* a matter and is why I placed its definition at the front of this book. You will be hearing me talk much of this word throughout these pages. In fact, you'll probably be sick of hearing about it by the time I'm done! A verse, if left to itself, could be interpreted in a variety of ways. However, when a subject is set, the verse must be interpreted within the confines of that subject. Sometimes the subject or context is set at the start of a chapter. Other times, it can be established at the beginning of a book. Whatever the case, it is the *only* legitimate way to discern the truth.

Here in Thessalonians, context plays a vital role. As you can see, I Thessalonians 5:1 is in *context* with I Thessalonians 4:16-17. The apostle Paul (the author of the letter) has already established the context and is still addressing the *rapture* subject. He's stating: "But of the times and the seasons [*concerning the afore mentioned rapture*], I have no need to tell you anything." Why? Let's read verse 2:

I Thessalonians 5:2
For yourselves know perfectly that the day of the Lord so cometh as a thief in the night.

This is an extremely important verse because Paul first describes the *rapture* of the church in I Thessalonians 4:16-17 and then, *through the avenue of context,* refers to that *rapture* event as the "day of the Lord" in I Thessalonians 5:2. This reveals that the "catching away" of the present day church is actually to occur on a day that is known to the apostle Paul as the *day of the Lord*.

There is much evidence to support this important relationship in other parts of the Bible. The most notable is found in the Old Testament book of Joel. Joel was a minor prophet with a major message. In fact, his entire book strictly concerns the coming day of the Lord. A study of Joel's writings easily verifies what Paul connected together in his letter.

Joel 2:11
*And the LORD shall **utter his voice** before his ar-*
my: for his camp is very great: for he is strong that
*executeth his word: for the **day of the LORD** is*
great and very terrible; and who can abide it?

Joel reveals that the Lord will utter His voice *on* the day
of the Lord. In his next chapter, it's addressed one more
time.

Joel 3:15-16
15Multitudes, multitudes in the valley of decision: for
*the **day of the LORD** is near in the valley of de-*
cision.
*16The LORD also shall roar out of Zion, and **utter***
***his voice** from Jerusalem; and the heavens and the*
earth shall shake: but the LORD will be the hope of
his people, and the strength of the children of Israel.

Twice, Joel states that the Lord will utter his voice *on*
the day of the Lord. With a return to the famous *rapture*
passage for comparison, an evident similarity becomes
immediately apparent:

I Thessalonians 4:16 – 5:2
*16For the **Lord** himself shall descend from heaven*
***with a shout**,...*
*2For yourselves know perfectly that the **day of the***
***Lord** so cometh as a thief in the night.*

As can be clearly seen, the same format and the same
terminology is being utilized here. It's a certain formula of
information merely being repeated by Paul: The Lord (Christ) will utter His voice *on* the day of the Lord. Paul was

simply living in an era that had already manifested the Messiah and knew that the Lord being referenced in the book of Joel that hadn't yet been revealed in Joel's day was none other than *Jesus Christ*.

Immediately, some try to make the case that Joel was referring to Yahweh/Jehovah (our Heavenly Father) and not to Jesus Christ and that Christ's shout of I Thessalonians 4 (along with the *rapture* of the church) is to be categorized separately from the Lord associated with the day of Jehovah spoken of in Joel's prophecy. *This separation directly conflicts with the words of Jehovah Himself.* To understand this concept with sharper clarity, a look at a citation made by Paul in his letter to the Romans is needed first.

Romans 11:26
*And so all Israel shall be saved: as it is written, There shall come out of **Sion the Deliverer**, and shall turn away ungodliness from Jacob:*

In relaying information to the Romans concerning the Second Coming of Christ, Paul directly quotes from the following verse found in the book of Isaiah:

Isaiah 59:20
*And the **Redeemer** shall come to Zion, and unto them that turn from transgression in Jacob, saith the LORD.*

According to Paul, the Redeemer mentioned in Isaiah is a specific reference to Jesus Christ. The significance of this truth is revealed in Isaiah 49:26.

Isaiah 49:26
And I will feed them that oppress thee with their own
flesh; and they shall be drunken with their own blood,
*as with sweet wine: and all flesh shall know that **I the***
LORD (Jehovah) am thy Saviour and thy Re-
deemer (Jesus Christ), the mighty One of Ja-
cob.

It is God-Jehovah Himself who claims to be that very Redeemer! The truth is, Jesus Christ is an extension of Jehovah and was Jehovah manifested in the flesh when He walked the earth 2000 years ago! This is why Jesus told His disciples: "he that hath seen Me hath seen the Father" (John 14:8) and also: "I and My Father are one" (John 10:30). This is just a small drop in a very large bucket of instances where Jehovah and Jesus Christ are described synonymously in Scripture; however, these initial examples provide excellent confirmation that the "Lord" portrayed in Isaiah and in the book of Joel _is_ Jesus Christ from the perspective of not only the apostle Paul, but *Jehovah Himself.*

When relaying the *rapture* doctrine to the Thessalonians, it is now more apparent that Paul merely carried this perspective from the book of Romans into his letter to the Thessalonians. He merely elaborated on the Old Testament further by simply applying the presently manifested Name of Jehovah—Jesus Christ (interpreted: Jehovah is salvation)—to Joel's original prophecy. It's the same technique he had clearly used in his letter to the Romans when identifying the Redeemer found in the Old Testament book of Isaiah as Jesus. This ultimately reveals that Christ is actually to be the one to utter His voice on the soon-coming day of the Lord. Since Paul also links the *rapture* of the church to this particular advent of Christ, then it's substantial confirmation that the *rapture* is to take place on the day of the Lord as well.

This becomes the first in a series of many additional proofs that Paul was indeed linking the *rapture* of the church to the day of the Lord, with multiple confirmations coming from the book of Joel. It also gives us an initial peek into where Paul is actually gathering his information from when establishing the *rapture* doctrine for the church. Throughout this book, you will begin to notice that he was merely referencing already-established truths, using both Christ and the Old Testament prophets as a guide. Realize, that prior to his conversion, Paul was a devout orthodox Jew and was well versed in Old Testament writings. In fact, he persecuted the early Christians because they chose to live by grace and not under the Mosaic Law like he was accustomed to. When he finally came to the truth of Christ, his well-grounded Old Testament upbringing allowed him to view prophecy in a whole new light, and when using Christ as the view finder, it gave him fresh insight concerning the end of the age. This, of course, included insight into the *rapture* of the church.

-Let us watch-

Beyond the Old Testament reference Paul makes concerning the Lord's shout, he continues his apparent connection between the *rapture* and the day of the Lord simply by how he addresses the Thessalonians in chapter 5. In I Thessalonians 5:2, he informs them that the day of the Lord will come as a thief in the night. The truth is, to interpret the remainder of the passage correctly, verse 2 must now be identified as the context-setter for the verses that follow. This is nothing more than a fundamental scriptural interpretation regulation, but it's immensely crucial to understand because in verse 4, Paul then reassures them that even though the day of the Lord is to come like a "thief in the night," that day will not overtake *them*—but why won't it?

> *I Thessalonians 5:5*
> *Ye are all the children of the light, and the children of the day...*

It's because they (we) are children of the day. Then he adds...

> Verse 6:
> *Therefore let us not sleep,... but let us watch,...*

The question that should be immediately asked here is: *Let us watch for what?* If taking into consideration the actual context in operation, Paul's statement in verse 6 is actually in direct reference to the context previously set in verse 2—ultimately revealing that it's the *day of the Lord* he wants the church to be watching for. Even though Paul began with a description of the *rapture,* he immediately provided a description concerning the day of the Lord with quick instruction to the church to be watching for *that* particular day. This fact, in and of itself, is an excellent source of confirmation that Paul was indeed linking the *rapture* and the day of the Lord together simply because he tells the church to watch for the day of the Lord in chapter 5 and not the *rapture.*

This is also a great foundational example in scriptural interpretation and its crucial relationship with context. If utilized in the correct manner, this key element simply allows the Bible to define itself. This easily obtainable yet necessary skill will open up the floodgates of knowledge and make your future studies more invigorating and much less complicated.

-Peter Confirms-

A great place to re-implement this vital skill is in the third chapter of II Peter. Here, the same day-of-the-Lord event Paul wrote about in I Thessalonians is further addressed by Peter the apostle.

> *II Peter 3:10-12*
> *¹⁰**But the day of the Lord will come as a thief in the night;** in the which the heavens shall pass away with a great noise, and the elements shall melt with fervent heat, the earth also and the works that are therein shall be burned up.*
> *¹¹Seeing then that all these things shall be dissolved, what manner of persons ought ye to be in all holy conversation and godliness,*
> *¹²**Looking for and hasting unto the coming of the day of God**, wherein the heavens being on fire shall be dissolved, and the elements shall melt with fervent heat?*

Peter sets up his passage in the same manner by first clarifying in verse 10 that he is speaking about the day of the Lord. *Again, this is to be recognized as the context-setter in relation to the remainder of the passage.* He then goes on to describe of how the heavens will pass away "with a great noise" and "melt with fervent heat" on that day. However, he immediately follows with a very important rhetorical question posed to the early church (paraphrased): *What kind of people should you be then, knowing that this particular day of God that you look for will come with such immense intensity?* (vs. 11-12) Clearly, Peter confirmed Paul's position simply by how Peter viewed the relationship of the church with the day of the Lord in his own day. Peter's rhetorical question undeniably reveals and unequivocally verifies that the early church *was* actually watching for the day of the Lord—just as Paul had instructed the Thessalonians to be doing! Peter immediately reaffirms this in verse 14 when he states: *Wherefore, beloved, seeing that ye look for such things...* Again, it is made abundantly clear that the infant church *did* have its eyes set on the day of the Lord. In just a few short verses later, Peter even goes so far as to remind the church that Paul was of the same mindset as he.

> *II Peter 3:15-16*
> *[15]And account that the longsuffering of our Lord is salvation; even as our beloved brother **Paul also, according to the wisdom given to him, wrote unto you;***
> *[16]**as also in all his epistles**, speaking in them of these things; wherein are some things hard to be understood, which the ignorant and unstedfast wrest, as they do also the other scriptures, unto their own destruction.*

Peter amplifies Paul's letter written to the Thessalonians, reminding the early church that Paul had offered up the exact same instructions to be watching for the soon-coming day of the Lord.

-When then?-

Up to this point, I have greatly emphasized the evident association between the *rapture* of the church and the day of the Lord for a particular reason because the significance is truly staggering. So what are the implications of this undeniable connection between these two stellar events? *Fortunately, the Bible is very specific about when the day of the Lord actually <u>begins</u>.* To determine this information, a study of the day of the Lord in the Old Testament is needed first. The first literal mention is found in the book of Isaiah.

Isaiah 13:9-10
*9Behold, the **day of the LORD** cometh, cruel both with wrath and fierce anger, to <u>lay the land desolate</u>: and he shall destroy the sinners thereof out of it.*
*10For the **stars of heaven** and the **constellations thereof shall not give their light**: the **sun shall be darkened** in his going forth, and the **moon shall not cause her light to shine**.*

As discussed earlier, the book of Joel is solely dedicated to the day of the Lord and mentions this particular day multiple times.

Joel 2:10-11
*10The earth shall quake before them; the heavens shall tremble: **the sun and the moon shall be dark, and the stars shall withdraw their shining**:*
*11And the LORD shall utter his voice before his army: for his camp is very great: for he is strong that executeth his word: for the **day of the LORD** is great and very terrible; and who can abide it?*

Joel 2:31
*The **sun shall be turned into darkness**, and the **moon into blood**, before the great and terrible **day of the LORD** come.*

Joel 3:14-15
*[14]Multitudes, multitudes in the valley of decision: for the **day of the LORD** is near in the valley of decision.*
*[15]The **sun and the moon shall be darkened**, and the **stars shall withdraw their shining**.*

And Zephaniah elaborates:

Zephaniah 1:14-15
*[14]The great **day of the LORD** is near, it is near, and hasteth greatly, even the voice of the day of the LORD: the mighty man shall cry there bitterly.*
*[15]That day is a day of wrath, a day of trouble and distress, a day of wasteness and desolation, **a day of darkness and gloominess, a day of clouds and thick darkness**,*

After reading these few passages, it becomes clearly evident that there is an obvious connection being made among all of these passages: *The sun and moon will be darkened, and the stars will withdraw their shining before (Joel 2:31) that day comes.* This information is of supreme importance because in Matthew chapter 24, these celestial events offer up a monumental clue in determining a timeline of end time events. There, Christ is informing His disciples about the end of the world and the signs that will precede His Second Coming.

Matthew 24:15,21,29

¹⁵*When ye therefore shall see the abomination of de-solation, spoken of by Daniel the prophet, stand in the holy place, (whoso readeth, let him understand:)*
²¹*For then shall be* **great tribulation**, *such as was not since the beginning of the world to this time, no, nor ever shall be.*
²⁹***Immediately after the tribulation*** *of those days shall the* **sun be darkened**, *and the* **moon shall not give her light**, *and the* **stars shall fall from heaven**, *and the powers of the heavens shall be shaken:*

An unmistakable correlation can be identified here! Christ just described the *exact* celestial events that are synonymous with the Old Testament day of the Lord! By informing His disciples that these specific astronomical signs are to occur immediately after the tribulation (the great tribulation), He also indirectly set a timeline for the day of the Lord—*it is to occur immediately after the great tribulation as well.* Of course, Christ's subtlety was intentional because He knew any basic student of Scripture would make the connection between these particular celestial events and the day of the Lord and thus embrace the day of the Lord as a post-tribulation event.

This connection is extremely important on many levels. First, it absolutely excludes the day of the Lord from occurring at anytime other than after the great tribulation period. I reiterate this fact because some try to portray this day as occurring throughout, and it is absolutely false. You won't find Scriptures encouraging you anywhere in this manner—I assure you! Again, it's extremely clear that the sun, moon, and stars will darken immediately after the great tribulation (that last half of Daniel's seventieth week) according to Matthew 24:29. Additionally, Joel clearly reveals in his prophecy that the day of the Lord *will not even come* until *after* this particular darkening of the sun, moon, and stars has been fulfilled (Joel 2:10,31). This leaves only one permissible starting point for the day of the Lord—*it can only begin sometime after the great tribulation.* In other words, the day of the Lord's arrival is wholly contingent upon the darkening of the sun, moon, and stars which, in and of itself, is a post-tribulation event according to Christ. This *requires* the day of the Lord to be a strict post-tribulation event.

This scriptural truth directly conflicts with those who might attempt to place the day of the Lord's starting point somewhere prior to the post-tribulation darkening of the sun, moon, and stars—for example, throughout Daniel's seventieth week. That is an impossible conclusion to be made according to Jesus Christ and Joel! The only way you could step around them is to claim that even though identical terminology is being utilized between the two passages, they are somehow speaking of two entirely separate blackouts. First, there's no scriptural evidence for this. Second, this mindset causes additional complications when crossing paths with Revelation 6:12 which, *again*, lists the exact same celestial events once more. Is the book of Revelation describing yet another full celestial blackout? Does God have an obsessive compulsion with the celestial light switch or does He only hit it once and then have His servants merely describe it from different prophetic aspects throughout the Bible? The first suggestion is highly improbable and counter-intuitive. The latter is the *simple,* logical choice.

Third, Jesus and Joel continued paralleling their prophecies beyond the mention of the celestial darkening of the sky. Both described God's wrath as an ensuing repercussion of this frightening cosmic episode as well (as does Revelation 6.) This further confirms the unity of these passages and showcases the fact that they are indeed speaking of an exclusive one-time celestial event which is merely being described from different prophetic angles.

Since Joel claims that the day of the Lord will not come until the sun, moon, and stars have first been darkened, and Christ's pivotal prophecy of Matthew 24:29 sets a clear and stringent post-tribulation timeline for this unique astronomical occurrence, then the day of the Lord must be acknowledged as a strict post-tribulation event.

-A True Capture of the Rapture-

Since Paul contextually links the *rapture* of I Thessalonians 4:16-17 with the day of the Lord just a few verses later in I Thessalonians 5:2. Since this is followed by instruction and warning coming from both Paul and Peter in their letters to the *present day church* to be watching for that particular day of the Lord (I Thess. 5:6, II Peter 3:11-12). Since this is matched with an obvious verification in II Peter 3:14 that the early church was indeed following this particular instruction unconditionally when Peter made the statement: *Seeing how you look for such things*—clearly referencing the day of the Lord previously described throughout his chapter, then the only astounding yet simple and logical conclusion that can be made is this:

THE RAPTURE OF THE PRESENT DAY CHURCH WILL NOT OCCUR UNTIL AFTER THE GREAT TRIBULATION ON THE GREAT DAY OF THE LORD.

One of the first major discrepancies to appear in the pre-tribulation *rapture* theory is found in their attempt to break the blaring context link between the *rapture* of the church and the day of the Lord (I Thess. 4:16-5:2) by placing the *rapture* on the end time timeline as an event that occurs seven years prior to that post-tribulation day. If this was truly the case, then why does the apostle Paul instruct the church to be watching for the day of the Lord in I Thessalonians 5:6—*a day set in stone by Scripture as a post-tribulation event*—if we are supposedly to be taken in a secret *rapture* seven years prior? Why does Peter make the assertion that the day of God Paul described to the Thessalonians, was the very same day the infant church was actually watching for at the time he wrote his letter? Wouldn't the hope in a pre-tribulation *rapture* of the church have nullified that belief? Wouldn't it make the instruction and warning of both Paul and Peter to be watching for the coming day of the Lord completely invalid? Why were they looking for the post-tribulation day of God instead? Why does John, in Revelation 1:7, when addressing the seven churches of his day—the, *then-known church world*—choose only to describe the powerful and most unmistakable post-tribulation return of Jesus Christ on the day of the Lord, of which, the *entire world* will witness and wail out in mournful anguish over? Yet, in doing so, he inexplicably fails to instill any hope about a gentle, behind-the-scenes secret pre-tribulation *rapture* which would simply be dismissed by the remaining global community as a "curious anomaly—unexplainable at this present moment"? Again, the simple, yet revealing, sobering, and most unavoidable fact remains: *because the church is to remain on earth until that particular post-tribulation day of the Lord comes!*

Since the great tribulation is an event that takes place

just prior to the day of the Lord, then the initial implications are that the church will witness the great tribulation period first hand—a concept that has, unfortunately, become inconceivable in the main stream church of today.

-*"One Will Be Taken"*-

Again, since Paul verifiably couples the *rapture* with the day of the Lord, and Christ, in Matthew 24, speaks of celestial events that are clearly synonymous with that particular day, a noticeable parallel begins to quickly form between the two of them when Jesus elaborates further about a large gathering that will take place on the day of the Lord after the sky turns black that only further validates Paul's position.

> *Matthew 24:29-31,40-41*
> [29]***Immediately after the tribulation of those days*** *shall the sun be darkened, and the moon shall not give her light, and the stars shall fall from heaven, and the powers of the heavens shall be shaken:*
> [30]*And then shall appear the sign of the Son of man in heaven: and then shall all the tribes of the earth mourn, and they shall see the Son of man coming in the clouds of heaven with power and great glory.*
> [31]*And he shall send his angels with a great sound of a trumpet, and they shall* ***gather together his elect*** *from the four winds, from one end of heaven to the other.*
> [40]*Then shall two be in the field; the* ***one shall be taken***, *and the other left.*
> [41]*Two women shall be grinding at the mill;* ***the one shall be taken***, *and the other left.*

Christ is unequivocally describing the *rapture* of believers here! Since this wreaks major havoc on the pretribulation *rapture* theory, an attempt has been made to distort this particular passage by claiming that those who are taken is an actual reference to the non-believers or "tares." This is extremely unlikely taking into consideration Matthew 24 in its entirety which begins with an eagerly asked question by the disciples to Jesus: *What will be the sign of your coming and the end of the world?* Jesus generously answered both questions by literally describing the signs that are to precede His Second Coming and then concluded with a vivid description of the return itself which, according to Christ, is to occur immediately after the great tribulation and is to *include the gathering of the elect at that time.*

From there, He immediately transitioned into the infamous parable of the fig tree—not to begin a new subject—but for the sole purpose of providing the disciples with a simple and easy identifiable illustration of how that particular post-tribulation return and the gathering of the elect is to unfold.

Matthew 24:32-33
32Now learn a parable of the fig tree; When his branch is yet tender, and putteth forth leaves, ye know that summer is nigh:
33So likewise ye, when ye shall see all these things, know that it is near, even at the doors.

It is to be emphasized that the "it" in verse 33 is a continued reference to the post-tribulation return of Christ *and also* to the gathering of the elect that is to occur on that same day. Of course, Christ foresaw the coming doctrinal controversies that would eventually encompass His return, reiterating the details again—but this time, from the perspective of Noah's day.

Matthew 24:37
But as the days of Noah were, so shall also the coming of the Son of man be.

Again, "the coming of the Son of man" is a continuation of the initial reference to His post-tribulation coming and to the connected gathering of the elect.

Matthew 24:38-41
38For as in the days that were before the flood they were eating and drinking, marrying and giving in marriage, until the day that Noe entered into the ark,
39And knew not until the flood came, and took them all away; so shall also the coming of the Son of man be.
*40Then shall two be in the field; the **one shall be taken**, and the other left.*
*41Two women shall be grinding at the mill; **the one shall be taken**, and the other left.*

I will acknowledge that, initially, it could be very easy to associate those taken away in the flood with "the one shall be taken," described just one verse later. But as I have been emphasizing, Jesus, just moments earlier, had literally and very specifically declared to His disciples that a *gathering of the elect* is to occur at the coming of the Son of man. Since the true intent of the Noah illustration was to merely elaborate on that original literal description, then those who are taken in verses 40 and 41 *must be* categorized with the elect who *must be* gathered at the coming of the Son of man according to Jesus. It is, by far, the most logical con-nection to be made when considering that the context is simply being carried from Christ's literal description over to the parable of the fig tree and finally into the comparison of Noah's day—where Noah (representative of today's believer) was the one who was actually *taken away* in salvation while the wicked were *left* to suffer the wrath of God in the great flood.

Fortunately for us, the disciples were as curious then as we are now and asked Jesus in Luke 17:37 to clarify what He was talking about when He used the word "taken."

Luke 17:37
And they answered and said unto him, Where, Lord? [where are they taken?] *And he said unto them, Wheresoever the body (carcass) is, thither will the eagles be gathered together.*

What cryptic message was Christ trying to relay? First, the word He used earlier for "taken" in the Greek translation is paralambano—a combination of para and lambano. It means: *To receive near or associate with one's self in any familiar intimate act or relation.* There is certainly nothing intimate between Christ and the unsaved so they cannot be the ones He was referring to. It is evident, when considering the Greek translation that Jesus was referring to the believers who, unarguably, have the intimate relationship with Him and who are to be taken at that time of His Second Coming.

Furthermore, the word "gathered" is associated with the eagles and that they aren't suffering in death, but are flying above it. In order to gather, you must take (not leave) and since the ones taken are the believers (because of their intimate connection with Christ), then the eagles are merely a representation of the true believers being gathered (*raptured*) when Christ returns. They are "caught up" or *taken* and follow Him to Jerusalem where Christ slaughters the armies gathered at Armageddon. That carnage will produce the carcasses, and we will witness this whole event from a literal bird's eye view! Where the carcass is (the unbeliever trodden down in God's wrath/Rev. 14:19-20), there the eagles will be gathered together! (believers caught up in the *rapture*.) Remarkable verification can be found in Matthew 24:27-31.

> *27For as the lightning cometh out of the east, and shineth even unto the west; so shall also the coming of the Son of man be.*
> *28For wheresoever the carcase is, there will the eagles be gathered together.*

The most common yet critical mistake made concerning the carcass/eagles mystery is that Christ is speaking literally when, in fact, He's speaking *symbolically*. This conclusion can be easily made with the realization that the above two verses are actually a quick overview of a more in depth description that immediately follows.

> *Matthew 24:30-31*
> *30And then shall appear the sign of the Son of man in heaven: and then shall all the tribes of the earth mourn, and they shall see the Son of man coming in the clouds of heaven with power and great glory.*
> *31And he shall send his angels with a great sound of a trumpet, and they shall gather together his elect from the four winds, from one end of heaven to the other.*

What many fail to recognize is that verses 30 and 31 are actually describing verse 27 and 28 in further detail. Christ immediately unlocks the mystery of His eagle analogy by producing the literal interpretation in the next few verses.

Matthew 24:27-28	Matthew 24:30-31
[27]For as the **lightning** cometh out of the east, and shineth even unto the west; so shall also the coming of the Son of man be. [28]For wheresoever the carcase is, there will the **eagles be gathered together.**	[30]And then shall appear the **sign** of the Son of man in heaven: and then shall all the tribes of the earth mourn, and they shall see the Son of man coming in the clouds of heaven with power and great glory. [31]And he shall send his angels with a great sound of a trumpet, and they shall **gather together his elect** from the four winds, from one end of heaven to the other.

First, the sign Jesus is referring to in verse 30 comes into focus when placing the verses side by side for comparison. It will come in the form of an unmistakable and unmatchable brilliant light extending from one side of the sky to the other *like perpetual lightning.* The source of this streaming light will be a projection of Christ's unbridled glory (and also from the inhabitants of heaven that follow) as He descends from the heavens onto earth.

On a quick side note, this is *extremely crucial* information for any believer who finds himself within the great tribulation period since deception will reign supreme just prior to the return of Christ. Many will be claiming that He's already on earth and in hiding, offering up various locations to His whereabouts. True believers will recognize these claims as being fraudulent because they will be apprised of the information presented here—that His return is actually to be accompanied by a unique light show, witnessed by the entire globe all at once, and irreproducible by any other.

However, it is the second set of verses (28 & 31) that reveals yet again who is actually to be taken at this critical point in time: *It is the elect*. As you can see, the word "gather" is associated with the eagles *and* the elect and showcases the eagles as a mere representation of the elect being gathered (taken) on that day. *see page 226.*

Put all of this information together, and it becomes extremely evident that Christ is describing Paul's *rapture* event verbatim; it's like He's reading from I Thessalonians chapters 4 and 5! The truth is, Paul, in his letter to the Thessalonian church regarding the *rapture*, is merely recapping Christ's prophecy of Matthew chapter 24. He even admits to the Thessalonians where He's getting his information from!

I Thessalonians 4:15
For this we say unto you by the word of the Lord...

I Thessalonians 4:16-5:7	Matthew 24:30-49
[16]For the **Lord himself shall descend from heaven with a shout...**	[30]...and they shall see the **Son of man coming in the clouds of heaven...**
...with the **voice of the archangel...**	[31]And he shall send his **angels**...
...and with the **trump of God...**	...with a **great sound of a trumpet...**
[17]Then we which are alive and remain shall be **caught up**...	...and they shall **gather together his elect**...
[5:4]But ye, brethren, are not in darkness, that that day should overtake you as a **thief.**	[43]...if the goodman of the house had known in what watch the **thief** would come...
[6]Therefore let us not sleep, as do others; but let us **watch** and be sober.	[42]**Watch** therefore: for ye know not what hour your Lord doth come.
[7]For they that sleep sleep in the night; and they that be **drunken** are drunken in the...	[49]And shall begin to smite his fellowservants, and to eat and drink with the **drunken**;...

Believe me, I am, in no way, trying to be rude by making the following statement, rather, I'm merely making an attempt to inject some much-needed perspective: *To say these two passages aren't fully related is absolute and utter foolishness.* However, to fully take hold of these evident parallels is to once again utilize the critical element of simplicity. It is this key element that will allow you to absorb the truth and see it for what it really is. If you still decide to ignore it, how much would you have to twist and turn your cranium to claim these passages are actually speaking of two entirely different events? Pre-tribulation proponents see the similarities yet still make an attempt at this contortionist act by attacking trivial words like "angels," "trump," "the," and "a" because they *have to* separate the day of the Lord from the *rapture* or they know their whole theory will unravel before them. However, this requires a complete disregard for the multitude of evident parallels being revealed between Christ's description and Paul's writing. The danger is, this can easily be accomplished when you decide the answer you were looking for does not include a persecution of the present day church by the Antichrist and begin searching for alternate "pop-ups" to help ease your mind even though the truth is staring right at you!

Even beyond the seven most obvious parallels seen here, there's an eighth and more obscure clue that can be found: *The day of the Lord*. Matthew 24:29 clearly describes celestial events that are to occur on that particular day, indirectly setting the day of the Lord event as the actual context in operation there. Paul, in his letter, comes right out and uses the term and connects the final parallel between the *rapture* passage of I Thessalonians and Matthew 24:29.

I Thessalonians 5:2
*For yourselves know perfectly that the **day of the Lord** will come as a thief...*

Curiously, pre-tribulation advocates acknowledge that this verse actually parallels Matthew 24, but still try to disconnect all the others Paul clearly makes in his passage. However, that doesn't nullify the fact that all the other parallels still remain, providing the much-needed proof of an undeniable relationship between I Thessalonians 4 and 5 and Matthew 24 as a whole. While Paul was initially careful to establish the *rapture* as a post-tribulation day-of-the-Lord event on his own through the simple use of context, the clear relationship between his passage and the very words of Christ in Matthew 24 only confirms it further.

-*Further Revelation*-

Revelation chapters 6 and 7 offer up even more scriptural proof that only further verifies the end time position of the church *rapture,* beginning with a study of the sixth seal in the twelfth verse. Here, another encounter with increasingly familiar terminology presents itself yet again.

> *Revelation 6:12-13*
> *12And I beheld when he had opened the sixth seal, and, lo, there was a great earthquake; and the **sun became black** as sackcloth of hair, and the **moon became as blood**;*
> *13And the **stars of heaven fell** unto the earth, even as a fig tree casteth her untimely figs, when she is shaken of a mighty wind.*

The first parallel is now easy to identify. The same information given by Christ in Matthew 24:29 and the Old Testament descriptions concerning the day of the Lord are stated again here: Sun darkened, moon as blood, and stars falling. Again, Jesus reveals that this particular celestial darkening of the sky will not occur until immediately after the tribulation. Therefore, this critical information sets a strict timeline for the rest of the events contained within the sixth seal; *they too, <u>must</u> occur immediately after the great tribulation.* With that in mind, a further dissection of the sixth seal begins to unravel a familiar message originally relayed by both Christ and Paul. What else does the sixth seal reveal?

Revelation 6:15-17
15And the kings of the earth, and the great men, and the rich men, and the chief captains, and the mighty men, and every bondman, and every free man, hid themselves in the dens and in the rocks of the mountains;
*16And said to the mountains and rocks, Fall on us, and hide us from the face of him that sitteth on the throne, and from the **wrath of the Lamb**:*
*17For the **great day of his wrath is come;** and who shall be able to stand?*

The first important item to be harvested from this text is that the *day of Christ* is beginning to take place and is again being described as a post-tribulation event—just as it is in Matthew 24. This can also be verified in Luke 17:30—a repeat passage of Matthew 24—where the day of the Lord is "the day when the Son of man is revealed." The "Son of man" is, of course, a reference to Jesus Christ, thus uniting the Old Testament day of the Lord with the day of Christ once again.

More evidence of this relationship can be found in the book of Isaiah which unfurls a description of the Old Testament day of the Lord (Jehovah) that mimics the one found at the sixth seal.

Isaiah 2:12,19
*12For the **day of the LORD** of hosts shall be upon every one that is proud and lofty, and upon every one that is lifted up; and he shall be brought low:*

*¹⁹And they shall go into the **holes of the rocks, and into the caves of the earth**, for fear of the LORD, and for the glory of his majesty, when he ariseth to shake terribly the earth.*

When the day of the Lord (Jehovah) finally arrives, unbelievers will scramble in sheer terror like cockroaches scurrying from the beam of a flashlight. They will be looking for any place to hide their wickedness from the wrath of God that they know is now inevitable. Unfortunately, this beam will be inescapable. The significance "in light" of the topic I am presenting is that this Old Testament description is *absolutely identical* to the description found at the sixth seal (Rev. 6:15-16)—a day that is now specifically being attributed to the Lamb (Christ). This further validates that the day of the Lamb (Christ) *is* the day of the Lord (Jehovah) incarnate.

This evident union is important on many levels. First, while Jehovah made it clear to Isaiah that He is also Jesus Christ—the Redeemer (Isaiah 49:26), it is now made clear here in Revelation that the day of Jehovah and the day of Christ are to be identified singularly as well. Second, because the apostle John reveals the day of the Lamb (Christ) to be the manifesting power of the Old Testament day of the Lord through his use of Isaiah's prophecy in chapter 2 verse 19 at the sixth seal, this fact absolutely legitimizes the relationship between Paul's letter to the Thessalonians concerning the *rapture* and Joel's prophecy of Joel 2:11. Like the apostle John, Paul *also utilized the Old Testament* and clearly attributed Christ's day of descent from the heavens (and the *rapture* of the church) to the Lord mentioned in the Old Testament book of Joel who is set to utter His voice on the day of the Lord. Third, it begins to showcase the evident similitude between Paul's *rapture* passage and the sixth seal of Revelation, proving that both Apostles adhered to the same viewpoint. It confirms that Paul was indeed contextually linking the day that Christ descends to the post-tribulation day of the Lord event (I Thess. 5:2) *because it's exactly what John does at the sixth seal.* This ultimately reveals that I Thessalonians 4:16 is, in fact, paralleling the post-tribulation sixth seal and further exposes a post-tribulation *rapture* of the present day church.

-*The Great Multitude*-

Fortunately, the apostle John provided authenticity. A continuation into the seventh chapter of Revelation reveals a parenthetical passage between the sixth and seventh seals which was designed to simply readdress certain aspects of the seals only from the perspective of the elect. First, Revelation 7:1 describes four angels at the four corners of the earth who are commanded to withhold destruction upon the earth momentarily. Then, in verse 2, another angel <u>ascends</u> from the east with the seal of God in his hand and is found to be the one issuing the command. Since Revelation 7 is indeed parenthetical, then understanding where to place the depicted events in relation to the seals is the next step. This is accomplished by searching for parallels in other areas of Scripture.

The fact that the fifth angel is <u>ascending</u> and not descending indicates that this particular angel will be on earth at this particular moment and will rise with a resounding shout or command issued to the four angels positioned at the four corners of the earth to withhold their destruction momentarily. Fortunately, in the book of Daniel, this angel is addressed by name.

Daniel 12:1-2
*¹And at that time shall Michael **stand up**, the great prince which standeth for the children of thy people: and there shall be a time of trouble, such as never was since there was a nation even to that same time: and at that time thy people shall be delivered, every one that shall be found written in the book.*
²And many of them that sleep in the dust of the earth shall awake, some to everlasting life, and some to shame and everlasting contempt.

The Greek word for "stand up" is "amad" which is also defined as "to arise." This perfectly mirrors the actions of the angel found in Revelation chapter 7 and begins an important connection between Revelation 7 and Daniel 12. Continuing with Daniel's prophecy, once Michael's ascension occurs, a time of trouble will ensue that has not been previously matched up to that point in history. That time of trouble is, of course, speaking of the great tribulation period (see Matt. 24:21). Therefore, according to Daniel's prophecy, Michael's ascension is to occur prior to the great tribulation.

When carrying this critical piece of information back to the book of Revelation, it becomes crystal clear that the events of Revelation chapter 7:1-8 (the 4 angels, Michael's ascension, and the sealing of the 144,000) actually reverse gears chronologically and occur just prior to the great tribulation period. They must be placed somewhere <u>before</u> the unloosing of the post-tribulation sixth seal (even though the sixth seal had just been addressed). This is when the first fruits of God—the 144,000—are sealed by the four angels at the four corners of the earth which will provide them with supernatural protection to prophesy boldly, without hindrance, throughout the great tribulation against the Beast system and its Antichrist figure.

However, it is <u>after</u> the pre (great) tribulation sealing of the 144,000, that John witnesses one other spectacular event:

Revelation 7:9
*After this I beheld, and, lo, **a great multitude**, which no man could number, of all nations, and kindreds, and people, and tongues, stood before the throne, and before the Lamb, clothed with white robes, and palms in their hands;*

There has been much speculation to the identity of this group and how they arrived before the throne. The key to understanding who they are and what occurs here is to simply continue following the parallel between Daniel 12 and Revelation 7. What is found after Michael's ascension and the great tribulation period is that Daniel 12:2 goes on to describe *a resurrection of both believers and unbelievers.* Although it wasn't revealed to Daniel in his day, the book of Revelation would reveal hundreds of years later precisely when these events are to take place. First, the resurrection of the just is to occur at Christ's Second Coming *after* the great tribulation but just *prior to* Christ's 1000 year rule on earth. This is recognized as the first resurrection (Rev. 20:6). Second, there is actually to be a 1000 year time gap between the resurrections of the just and of the unjust because it's clear that the resurrection of the unjust doesn't occur until 1000 years later—after Christ's millennial reign on earth. This is portrayed in Revelation 20:13.

Since the resurrection of the <u>just</u> is clearly listed as a post-tribulation/pre-millennial event in Revelation 20, and Daniel 12:2 is merely a parallel passage to that event, then the resurrection of believers depicted in Daniel 12:2 is to be interpreted as a post-tribulation/pre-millennial event as well. Likewise, since Revelation 7 is also paralleling Daniel 12, then the great multitude—witnessed by John the apostle—is none other than the *post-tribulation/pre-millennial resurrection of believers* (also making it a parallel to the resurrection of Rev. 20:6).

It's clear, when comparing the two passages, that Daniel describes the ascension of an angel and then follows it almost immediately with a description concerning the resurrection of true believers. John follows an identical format in Revelation 7 by also describing the ascension of an angel, with a description of a large gathering of believers occurring soon after. Again, it's the post-tribulation/pre-millennial resurrection.

Simply studying the resurrection solely from the perspective of Revelation 7, it's apparent that this immeasurable multitude didn't file into God's presence over any extended period of time, but actually appeared all at once and in unison, providing even more indications of an instantaneous resurrection. Second, they are standing before God with palms in their *hands*—demonstrating that they have *bodies*. The only way this could be a possibility is if the resurrection of the just had just occurred which would reunite earthly bodies with the souls that had left them previously. It should also be noted that the martyrs are set aside by Scripture and specifically addressed at the fifth seal—a timeframe that encompasses the great tribulation period, rendering a duplicate depiction of the martyrs at Revelation 7:9 highly unlikely.

In relation to the timing, one of the elders in John's vision asks John if he knows where this vast group appeared from:

Revelation 7:14
And I said unto him, Sir, thou knowest. And he said
*to me, **These are they which came out of great***
***tribulation,** and have washed their robes, and*
made them white in the blood of the Lamb.

The elder informs the apostle that they came <u>out</u> of great tribulation—an undeniable proof that they were <u>in</u> great tribulation prior to their arrival before the throne of God. This confirms the post-tribulation timeframe of this instantaneous gathering.

So again, who is this vast and diverse group of people depicted in Revelation 7:9? The answer is that John, under revelation of God, has actually just witnessed the infamous resurrection of the just. This unique one-time event occurs after the great tribulation according to Daniel 12 and to the firsthand account given by the elder of John's vision, and on the day of the Lord/Lamb *prior to* Christ's millennial reign on earth according to the sequence of events listed in Revelation 19 and 20. (Remember, Rev. 19/20 is paralleling Daniel 12 also.)

Since Revelation 7 is a parenthetical passage set outside the seals to describe end time events from the perspective of the elect, then where does this resurrection take place in relation to all seven seals? The only seal to represent both a post-tribulation timeframe (because of its depiction of Matthew 24:29's post-tribulation cosmic events), and the day of the Lord/Lamb adequately enough (Rev. 6:17) is the <u>*sixth seal*</u>. Therefore, in relation to the seven seals, this monumental resurrection event must occur at the post-tribulation sixth seal on the day of Jehovah and of the Lamb.

What many fail to recognize is that this post-tribulation day-of-the-Lord "first resurrection" of the just, depicted in

Revelation 7:9, is the *exact same resurrection* that Paul was referring to in his famous *rapture* passage of I Thessalonians 4:16. The major clue points yet again back to the inescapable context link between the resurrection of true believers of I Thessalonians 4:16, and the post-tribulation day of the Lord, found just a few verse later in I Thessalonians 5:2—*just as Revelation describes it to be at the unloosing of the post-tribulation sixth seal.* Since Paul also clearly lists the *rapture* of the church to take place after this particular resurrection, then the *rapture* of the church must be acknowledged as a post-tribulation event as well.

-*The Pivotal Isaiah Text*-

However, the apostle Paul was not satisfied with leaving any of these truths to chance. In I Corinthians 15 (another area of Scripture that has been wholeheartedly accepted by pre-tribulation believers as an another reference to the pre-tribulation *rapture* of the church), Paul writes his first letter to a shaky church in Corinth to, among other reasons, reestablish the resurrection and *rapture* doctrine which had become severely compromised by claims that a resurrection from the dead was impossible. This passage repeats portions of its sister Scripture by again describing the trumpet sound, resurrection of the dead, and the *rapture.*

I Corinthians 15:51-52
*⁵¹Behold, I shew you a mystery; We shall not all sleep, but we shall all be **changed**,*
*⁵²In a moment, in the twinkling of an eye, at the last trump: for the trumpet shall sound, and the dead shall be raised incorruptible, and we shall be **changed**.*

However, it is in I Corinthians 15:54, just two verses later, that a crucial yet severely overlooked piece of evidence concerning its timing is found.

I Corinthians 15:54
So when this corruptible shall have put on incorruption, and this mortal shall have put on immortality, then shall be brought to pass the saying that is written, **Death is swallowed up in victory.**

Close to the completion of his description to the Corinthians concerning the *rapture* of the church, Paul takes the time to describe one last important aspect of the event to help unravel its mysteries a little further—"death is swallowed up in victory." It seems that the tables will eventually turn on poor old death which will get a debilitating dose of its own medicine. Being consumed forever, the catching away of the church will be the event that places the final proverbial nail in death's coffin.

But a quick search reveals that Paul is actually quoting an Old Testament prophet—citing part of a verse found in the book of Isaiah.

Isaiah 25:8
He will **swallow up death in victory***; and the Lord GOD will wipe away tears from off all faces; and the rebuke of his people shall he take away from off all the earth: for the LORD hath spoken it.*

What becomes of particular interest is the context that surrounds this verse. Going back one chapter reveals this information.

Isaiah 24:21-23
²¹*And it shall come to pass in that **day**, that the **LORD** shall punish the host of the high ones that are on high, and the kings of the earth upon the earth.*
²²*And they shall be gathered together, as prisoners are gathered in the pit, and shall be shut up in the prison, and after many days shall they be visited.*
²³*Then the **moon shall be confounded, and the sun ashamed**, when the LORD of hosts shall reign in mount Zion, and in Jerusalem, and before his ancients gloriously.*

By now, this should be sounding vaguely familiar. These few verses are speaking about the <u>day of the Lord</u> (Isaiah 13:9-10) of which, during that time, will be conjoined with a total blackout of the heavens. Again, Christ tells His disciples in Matthew 24:29 that this particular heavenly event will not, in any way, occur until after the great tribulation.

It is immediately after Isaiah's description concerning the day of the Lord, however, that the tone changes in chapter 25 from destruction of the wicked, to victory for the righteous, *and is exactly where Paul's rapture parallel rests!*

Isaiah 24, 25

In that day, that the LORD shall punish the host of the high o[...] are on high, and the king[s ...] earth upon the earth. [2]A[...] shall be gathered together, [...] oners are gathered in the [...] shall be shut up in the prison, and after many days shall they be visited. [23]Then the moon shall be confounded, and the sun ashamed, when the LORD of hosts shall reign in mount Zion, and in Jerus[...] and before his ancients glo[...] ly. [1]O Lord, thou art my God; [...] exalt thee, I will praise thy nam[e ...] thou hast done wonderful t[...] thy counsels of old are faithf[ul ...] and truth. [2]For thou hast mad[e ...] city an heap; of a defenced [...] ruin: a palace of strangers to [...] city; it shall never [...] built.[3]Therefore shall the s[...] people glorify thee, the city [...] terrible nations shall fear thee...[8]He will swallow up death in victory; and the Lord GOD will wipe away tears from off all faces; and the rebuke of his people shall he take away from off all the earth: fo[r ...] LORD hath spoken it.[9]And it sh[...] said in that day, Lo, this is our [...] we have waited for him, and h[...] save us: this is the LORD; we [...] waited for him, we will be gla[d ...] rejoice in his salvation.

"Then the moon shall be confounded and the sun ashamed"

Parallel:

Matthew 24:29

[29]**Immediately after the tribulation** of those days shall the **sun be darkened, and the moon shall not give her light, and the stars shall fall from heaven**, and the powers of the heavens shall be shaken:

Paul's citation of Isaiah 25:8, used in establishing the rapture doctrine for the church, is found here:
"He will swallow up death in victory"

Parallel: I Corinthians 15:54

First, it can be safely assumed that Isaiah is still in context with the post-tribulation day of the Lord event at this critical *rapture* juncture because five verses beyond Paul's citation, we still find ourselves "In that day."

Isaiah 26:1
In that day (the day of the Lord) *shall this song be sung in the land of Judah; We have a strong city; salvation will God appoint for walls and bulwarks*

What has to be taken into immediate consideration is this: If Paul was truly advocating a pre-tribulation *rapture* of the church in I Corinthians 15, declaring a completely separate and unique doctrine from all of the preceding Holy Prophets and also from Jesus Christ Himself, then why does he try to propagate it by citing a verse that, in regard to context, is strictly post-tribulation in nature? The answer is that *Paul was never a pre-tribulation rapture believer to begin with.* Paul's use of Isaiah 25:8 is immensely critical for many reasons, but primarily, it recaptures and solidifies Paul's belief in the binding relationship between the *rapture* of the church and the day of the Lord. Just as he had informed the Thessalonians that the *rapture* will not occur until that day, he completely verifies it by his utilization of Isaiah's prophecy in his *rapture* description to the Corinthian church which is again clearly in context with that same day.

However, the significance of Isaiah 25:8 continues. While it's undeniable that Paul clearly utilized the verse to establish the *rapture* doctrine for the church, what also becomes quickly undeniable is that the apostle John also quoted from the *exact same verse,* copying a subsequent phrase nearly word for word. This can be found in Revelation 7.

Revelation 7:9,17
*⁹After this I beheld, and, lo, a **great multitude**, which no man could number,...*
*¹⁷**and God shall wipe away all tears from their eyes.*** *(Isaiah 25:8 - God shall wipe away all tears from their eyes)*

Again, what becomes immediately and particularly interesting is the context surrounding John's use of Isaiah 25:8. In amazing replica fashion, John, in describing the gathering of "a great multitude," not only directly quotes from the same Old Testament verse Paul used to establish the *rapture* doctrine for the church, but as seen in the diagram on the following page, he also copies and reinforces the post-tribulation context of Isaiah's passage as well!

Revelation 6,7

[12]And I beheld when he had opened the sixth seal, and, lo, there was a great earthquake; and the **sun became black** as sackcloth of hair, and the **moon became as blood**; [13]And the **stars of heaven fell** unto the earth, even as a fig tree casteth her untimely figs, when she is shaken of a mighty wind... [17]For the great day of his wrath is come;... [1]And after these things I saw four angels standing on the four corners of the earth,... [4]And I heard the number of them which were sealed: and there were sealed an hundred and forty and four thousand [9]After this I beheld, and, lo, **a great multitude**, which no man could number, of all nations, and kindreds, and people, and tongues, stood before the throne, and before the Lamb... [14]These are they which came out of great tribulation, and washed their robes and made white in the blood of the Lamb [16]They shall hunger no more, neither thirst any more; neither shall the sun light on them, nor any heat. [17]For the Lamb which is in the midst of the throne shall feed them, and shall lead them unto living fountains of waters: and **God shall wipe away all tears from their eyes.**

"...and the sun became black as sackcloth of hair, and the moon became as blood; [13]And the stars of heaven fell..."

Parallel:

Matthew 24:29
[29]**Immediately after the tribulation** of those days shall the **sun be darkened, and the moon shall not give her light, and the stars shall fall from heaven**, and the powers of the heavens shall be shaken:

John's citation of Isaiah 25:8, used in relation to the great multitude, is found here:

"God shall wipe away all tears from their eyes."

This makes Isaiah 25:8 extremely invaluable because first and most importantly, it provides a scripturally-legitimate passageway between Paul's *rapture* passage of I Corinthians 15:52 and the great multitude of Revelation 7. This primarily reveals that both the apostle Paul and the apostle John are speaking of the *exact same event* and that the resurrection and *rapture* of the church is indeed being depicted in Revelation 7:9 contrary to all the diverse theories surrounding that group of people.

Second, since the event of the great multitude takes place at the sixth seal—on the post-tribulation day of the Lord and of the Lamb, it brings us once again to the inescapable and unavoidable (and reoccurring) truth that Paul's *rapture* of I Corinthians 15:51 is to be interpreted as a post-tribulation event from the perspective of not only the apostle John in Revelation, but again, since John and Paul both directly quote from Isaiah 25:8—a verse that is *also* set in a strict post-tribulation context—then from the perspective of the Prophet Isaiah as well.

Third, while some try to portray Paul as a lone pioneer of the church *rapture* doctrine, both Apostles' convergence on Isaiah 25:8 to describe a soon-coming large gathering of believers reveals that both Apostles adhered to the same post-tribulation viewpoint established by yet another Prophet many centuries earlier. *Paul was merely reiterating already-established Old Testament truths when imparting the rapture doctrine to the church.* Just as he had extracted information from Joel's prophecy to inform the Thessalonians of the *rapture*, he decides to utilize the well-established prophecies of Isaiah to relay the exact same information to the Corinthian church—that the church will not see *rapture* salvation until the great post-tribulation day of the Lord.

-Simplifying the Equation-

I have taken the liberty of boiling this entire chapter down into a much easier-to-digest formula. I urge you to study the following at length.

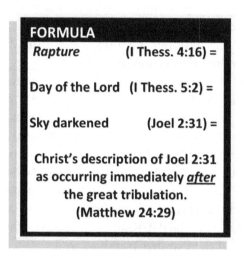

FORMULA

Rapture   (I Thess. 4:16) =

Day of the Lord (I Thess. 5:2) =

Sky darkened   (Joel 2:31) =

Christ's description of Joel 2:31 as occurring immediately _after_ the great tribulation. (Matthew 24:29)

To conclude, the most important thing to reap from this chapter is that the *rapture* of the present day church is to take place *on* the day of the Lord. The Apostles always associated Christ's <u>next</u> return with this particular day.

Second, the day of the Lord is clearly presented, both in the Old and New Testament, as a day that can only come about after the great tribulation. There has been much confusion (speculation) that this particular day encompasses the entire tribulation period and it's just not scriptural.

Third, the "day of the Lord" and the "day of Christ" are synonymous.

Fourth; Daniel 12, Joel 2, Matthew 24, <u>I Corinthians 15, I Thessalonians 4</u>, and Revelation 6 are all talking about the same resurrection event which in every instance is always associated with the post-tribulation day of the Lord either directly or indirectly. Daniel refers to the resurrection as an awakening and lists it to occur after the great tribulation (Dan. 12:2). Joel calls it an "army" and a "camp" and directly ties it to the day of the Lord (Joel 2:11). Jesus labels it a gathering and describes celestial events that are to occur on the day of the Lord (Matt. 24:29-31). For the Corinthians, Paul uses the terms "sleep" and "changed" and immediately quotes from a verse found in the Old Testament book of Isaiah that is in clear context with the day of the Lord. To the Thessalonians, he again describes it in a sleep/wake format (just as Daniel did) and blatantly links it the day of the Lord only a few verses later (I Thess. 4:16-5:2). Finally, John witnesses an instantaneous gathering of a great multitude being saved on the day of the Lord (Rev 7:9) and upon writing it down in great post-tribulation detail, also quotes from the exact Old Testament verse Paul used to establish the church *rapture* doctrine for the Corinthians.

That's *six* different areas of Scripture utilizing the same terminology and timeframe yet, curiously, a disconnection of I Corinthians 15 and I Thessalonians 4/5 is still attempted by many mainstream intellects. If Daniel 12, Joel 2, Matthew 24, and Revelation 6 can be accepted as interconnected, truly can a logical rejection of I Corinthians 15 and I Thessalonians 4 be feasible when they are making use of the same verses, terminology, and timing of all the other passages? The obvious and most logical answer is that I Corinthians 15 and Thessalonians 4 are both speaking of the post-tribulation resurrection, and the *rapture* of the present day church will not occur until the great day of the Lord arrives.

The Last Trump

Although a tremendous connection between the major *rapture* passage of I Corinthians 15:51 and the post-tribulation day of the Lord has now been identified, further investigation into this passage offers up even more post-tribulation evidence from the perspective of a trumpet that is to sound as this stellar event catches away the church.

> *I Corinthians 15:51-52*
> *51Behold, I shew you a mystery; We shall not all sleep, but we shall all be **changed**,*
> *52In a moment, in the twinkling of an eye, **at the last trump**: for the trumpet shall sound, and the dead shall be raised incorruptible, and we shall be **changed**.*

Unlike his letter to the Thessalonians, here, Paul becomes a little more specific with the trumpet sound associated with this mysterious event by labeling it the *last trump*. This small piece of information doesn't seem to be of great significance initially, but a deeper search into the Scriptures begins to light yet another path to the true timing of the *rapture.*

To begin, the Greek word for "trump" is salpigx (sal'-pinx) which literally means "to sound a trumpet." This Greek word is also utilized in the I Thessalonians 4 *rapture* passage.

> *I Thessalonians 4:16*
> *...with the trump* (salpigx) *of God...*

To get a better sense of when this final trumpet actually sounds, a search for the use of this particular Greek word in other areas of the Bible becomes the first logical step. A scan of the Scriptures quickly reveals it to be active in the book of Revelation as well.

> *Revelation 8:2*
> *And I saw the seven angels which stood before God; and to them were given seven **trumpets**. (salpigx)*

This match establishes an important connection between the particular trumpet Paul describes in I Corinthians and the seven trumpets of Revelation which only becomes clearer upon further investigation. Since Paul focuses on the last trumpet, then logic demands further study of any verses relating to the last of the seven trumpets in Revelation to see if there are any further similarities found between the two passages. The first mention is found in Revelation 10.

> *Revelation 10:7*
> *But in the days of the voice of the **seventh angel**, when he shall begin to sound, the **mystery of God** should be finished, as he hath declared to his servants the prophets.*

Here, the seventh angel sounds the last trumpet in the series of seven trumpets, and the "mystery of God" is "finished" when this particular sounding takes place.

To interpret this verse correctly in its entirety, the terms being offered must be defined correctly first. This is accomplished by adhering to another simple yet critical rule of scriptural interpretation—*Scripture defines Scripture.* This rule is just as important to utilize and is just as relevant as contextual interpretation because it always provides an objective definition of a term that is not dependent upon biased opinion. In the end, the true intent of the passage is allowed to stand out. By applying this principal to Revelation 10:7, how does Scripture define the term "mystery of God" elsewhere?

Ephesians 3:2-6
²If ye have heard of the dispensation of the grace of God which is given me to you-ward:
³How that by revelation he made known unto me the **mystery***; (as I wrote afore in few words,*
⁴Whereby, when ye read, ye may understand my knowledge in the **mystery of Christ***)*
⁵Which in other ages was not made known unto the sons of men, as it is now revealed unto his holy apostles and prophets by the Spirit;
*⁶**That the Gentiles should be fellowheirs, and of the same body, and partakers of his promise in Christ by the gospel***:*

Colossians 1:26-27
²⁶Even the **mystery** *which hath been hid from ages and from generations, but now is made manifest to his saints:*

*27To whom God would make known what is the riches of the glory of this **mystery among the Gentiles**; which is Christ in you, the hope of glory.*

Romans 11:25
*For I would not, brethren, that ye should be ignorant of this **mystery**, lest ye should be wise in your own conceits; that blindness in part is happened to Israel, **until the fulness of the Gentiles be come in**.*

After reading these passages, it becomes immediately clear that the mystery of God, hidden in past ages, is the Gentiles' inclusion into the *church* through faith in Jesus Christ. *The mystery of God is the present day church!*

This term is used many times throughout the New Testament and always relates to the church in every instance. For example:

What the church is based upon:

I Timothy 3:16
*And without controversy great is the **mystery of godliness**: God was manifest in the flesh, justified in the Spirit, seen of angels, preached unto the Gentiles, believed on in the world, received up into glory.*

How we enter the church:

Ephesians 1:3,5,9
3Blessed be the God and Father of our Lord Jesus Christ, who hath blessed us with all spiritual blessings in heavenly places in Christ:

⁵Having predestinated us unto the adoption of children by Jesus Christ to himself, according to the good pleasure of his will,
*⁹Having made known unto us the **mystery of his will**, according to his good pleasure which he hath purposed in himself:*

And of course, back to Revelation 10:7

*But in the days of the voice of the **seventh angel**, when he shall **begin to sound**, the **mystery of God** should be **finished**, as he hath declared to his servants the prophets*

Although many attempts have been made to redefine the "mystery of God" in this verse, it surely remains unchanged if the rules of scriptural interpretation are simply followed. Here, an important example of Scripture-defines-Scripture takes center stage because the "mystery of God" is clearly being defined in every other area of Scripture as a reference to the *present day church* in each instance. More importantly, it is to be *finished* in the days of the seventh angel according to Revelation 10:7.

To meddle with the "mystery of God" definition here would not only be contrary to the laws of scriptural interpretation, but also to the evident similarity that now manifests between the writings of Paul and John when adhering to this rule. When scriptural interpretation rules are respected, and the present day church is applied to the term "mystery of God" in Revelation just like it is throughout other New Testament books, it then begins to shed light on the perfect harmonization between Revelation 10:7 and the church *rapture* description Paul provides in I Corinthians 15—who *also* reveals a finalization of the church era at a last trumpet blast. This parallel only appears when honoring the Scripture-defines-Scripture rule yet shows that the term "mystery of God" is not connected to the last trumpet of Revelation by mere coincidence. Instead, it directly points to Paul's infamous *rapture* passage of I Corinthians 15:51. The apostle John was simply adhering to, and solidifying the truth of Paul's well-established doctrine!

This brings to mind the prevailing ideology that the church is not mentioned after Revelation 3. The "mystery of God" mentioned in Revelation 10 utterly debunks the *pre-three theory* (the belief that there's no mention of the church on earth after Revelation 3). I also urge those of you who hold to this concept to reconsider this verse:

> *I Corinthians 1:2*
> *Unto the church of God which is at Corinth, to them that are sanctified in Christ Jesus, **called to be saints**,*

The Bible clearly defines the word "saints" here. It is the *church* separated from the world in Christ Jesus. The word "saints" is associated with the church many times within the New Testament—the above verse being one of many examples. Revelation scatters the word all throughout its text and *especially* after the third chapter which means that within the safe confines of the Biblical definition of the word "saints," the word *church* can securely be applied as well. This is yet another prime example of Scripture defining Scripture.

-The Seventh Angel-

If the church is truly finished in the days of the seventh angel, then what takes place from the perspective of the apostle John when this angel sounds the final trumpet blast?

> *Revelation 11:15,18*
> *[15]And the seventh angel sounded; (his trumpet) and there were great voices in heaven, saying,* **The kingdoms of this world are become the kingdoms of our Lord, and of his Christ;** *and he shall reign for ever and ever.*
> *[18]And the nations were angry, and thy wrath is come, and* **the time of the dead,** *that they should be judged, and that thou shouldest give* **reward unto thy servants** *the prophets,* **and to the saints,** *and them that fear thy name, small and great; and shouldest* **destroy them which destroy the earth.**

It is revealed that when the seventh angel sounds the last of seven trumpets, the kingdoms of the world become the kingdoms of our Lord, God's wrath is come, the dead are judged, rewards are given to God's servants, and those who have destroyed the earth are they themselves destroyed. While the term "mystery of God" in Revelation 10:7 provides the initial evidence for a finalization of the church era "in the days of the seventh angel," the surrounding events finally revealed at this particular angel's last trumpet sound provides the remaining proof. The parallels are listed on the next page.

The Last Trumpet of I Corinthians	The Last Trumpet of Revelation
Kingdoms delivered up to God. (I Cor. 15:24)	Kingdoms of the world become the kingdoms of the Lord. (Rev. 11:15)
The dead shall be raised incorruptible. (I Cor. 15:52)	The time of the dead (Rev. 11:18)
Changed/*rapture* (I Cor. 15:52)	Rewards to the servants (Rev. 11:18)
Shall put down all rule and authority. (I Cor. 15:24)	Those who destroy the earth are destroyed (Rev. 11:18)

As you can see, many more parallels are revealed between the two passages, bringing us to the unavoidable conclusion that I Corinthians 15 and Revelation 11 are actually speaking of the exact same trumpet sound. This clear succession of parallels solidifies the relationship between the last trumpet of I Corinthians 15—the end of the church era—with the last trumpet of John's Revelation, ultimately revealing that the church is to be present on earth until the seventh trumpet blast where it is to be finally completed at that time.

-Daniel's Perspective-

The fact that the last trumpet of I Corinthians 15:52 and the last trumpet of Revelation 11:15 are clearly describing one singular event has staggering implications time-wise when taking into consideration all of the other invaluable prophecies found, not only within the book of Revelation, but within the book of Daniel as well. Many of Daniel's prophecies concern the time of the end. Here, the parallel develops.

Daniel 7:21-22, 26-27
21I beheld, and the same horn made war with the saints, and prevailed against them;
*22Until the Ancient of days came, and judgment was given to the saints of the most High; and the time came that the **saints possessed the kingdom**.*
26But the judgment shall sit, and they shall take away his (Satan/Antichrist's) dominion, to consume and to destroy it unto the end.
*27And the kingdom and dominion, and the greatness of the kingdom under the whole heaven, **shall be given to the people of the saints** of the most High, whose kingdom is an everlasting kingdom, and all dominions shall serve and obey him*

Verses 22 and 27 both plainly reveal that the kingdom of Satan is ultimately given to the "people of the saints." This is a *direct tie* to the last trumpet of Revelation 11:15 whereby we are told that the "kingdoms of this world are become the kingdoms of our Lord." Taking into consideration this initial parallel, an important factor begins to emerge in Daniel's passage in relation to the timing of this particular event upon further investigation. As you can see, *before* the saints are given the kingdom, Daniel writes that the "same horn" (Antichrist) made war with saints and prevailed against them.

First, for those unfamiliar with this particular individual, this Antichrist will be the end time ruler with the entire world at his disposal during the great tribulation just before Jesus returns. He will govern Satan's one world government in mockery of the true Christ. During that time, he will require everyone to wear his mark *in* their hands or *in* their foreheads (associated with the number 666) as an act of submission to his power and authority.

> *Revelation 13:16-17*
> ¹⁶*And he causeth all, both small and great, rich and poor, free and bond, to receive a mark in their right hand, or in their foreheads:*
> ¹⁷*And that no man might buy or sell, save he that had the mark, or the name of the beast, or the number of his name.*

Those who refuse this mark will be unable to buy or sell the everyday items they need to survive. They will be left outside of the system and ultimately hunted down and killed for treason. Presently, it's really not hard to imagine how easily this scenario could unfold under the right sinister leadership. Begin by simply pulling out your social security card! Without it, you're considered ineligible to receive the benefits entitled to American citizens. If you desire a job, a car, a house, or a credit line, you are required to provide this crucial number. If you do not comply, the system's eyes remain blind to your identity until you obtain a recognizable number that places you into that system. It is, of course, undeniable that this present system already dictates how today's society is managed, and is unfortunately a precursor to a darker future.

The Antichrist's mark will be similar to the social security number concept, except his system will encompass the globe and the penalty for non-compliance will be death. True believers will understand the significance of this mark and will refuse to bow to his authority. Revelation 14:9-10 tells us why...

Revelation 14:9-10
*⁹And the third angel followed them, saying with a loud voice, If any man worship the beast and his image, and **receive his mark in his forehead, or in his hand,***
*¹⁰**The same shall drink of the wine of the wrath of God**, which is poured out without mixture into the cup of his indignation; and he shall be tormented with fire and brimstone in the presence of the holy angels, and in the presence of the Lamb:*

Consequently, submission to the Beast and his system will be eternal separation from God. Therefore, true believers will defy the Antichrist throughout the course of the great tribulation—many losing their lives in the process. In this way, the Beast/Little-Horn/Antichrist will overcome the saints in a physical manner during this short period. Ironically, this physical overcoming of the saints will be the necessary catalyst needed in order for the saints to simultaneously overcome Satan *spiritually* (Revelation 12:11). While Satan may get a small amount of satisfaction in his short tyrannous rampage, his satisfaction will be pitifully miniscule in light of eternity where the saints will experience a perpetual state of victory long after he's gone.

As mentioned earlier, this information is of great significance because again, *before* the kingdom is possessed by the saints, Daniel reveals that they are to be *first* overcome by the Antichrist and his worldly system during the great tribulation. Even though I Corinthians 15 has become a cornerstone Scripture for the pre-tribulation *rapture* theory, the Bible actually places it at the seventh trumpet of Revelation due to the multitude of unavoidable parallels that manifest between the two passages. At the same time, Daniel places the seventh trumpet of Revelation, via parallel, on his own timeline as an event that will only come about after the great tribulation as well. Therefore, the conclusion that has to be made is that the last trump *rapture* of I Corinthians 15:51-53 cannot take place until after the great tribulation.

Daniel 7	I Corinthians 15	Revelation
Great Tribulation:	*These parallels prove the time-frame of Daniel's passage.*	**Great Tribulation:**
[21]I beheld, and the same horn made **war with the saints,** and prevailed against them;... [25] ...until **a time and times and the dividing of time.** (3.5 yrs)	*These parallels prove that the last trump of I Corinthians 15 is post-tribulation from the perspective of both Daniel & the book of Revelation.*	[13:5]...and power was given unto him to continue **forty and two months.** (3.5 yrs) [7]And it was given unto him to make **war with the saints,**...
Post-Tribulation:		**The Last Trumpet:**
[22]and the time came that **the saints possessed the kingdom.**	[24]Then cometh the end, when he shall have **delivered up the kingdom to God,**	[11:15]And the seventh angel sounded; ...**The kingdoms of this world are become the kingdoms of our Lord,**...
[22]Until the Ancient of days came, and **judgment was given to the saints...**	[52]...**for the trumpet shall sound, and the dead shall be raised incorruptible,**	[15]And the **seventh angel sounded;** (context) [18]...and the **time of the dead, that they should be judged,**
[26]...and they shall **take away his (Antichrist's) dominion,**	[24]...he shall have **put down all rule and all authority and power.**	[18]...**and shouldest destroy them which destroy the earth.**

-Isaiah's Perspective-

The last trumpet of I Corinthians 15:52 is quite troublesome for pre-tribulation proponents since the numerous parallels revealed between that passage and the last trumpet of Revelation are obvious to any casual reader of the Word. But perhaps the most compelling evidence for the timing of the last trumpet of I Corinthians 15:52 necessitates a return back to the crucial citation Paul makes at the end of his *rapture* description—found in I Corinthians 15:54. As discussed in full detail in the previous chapter, there, when establishing the *rapture* doctrine for the church, Paul clearly cites a portion of Isaiah 25:8 which, upon further investigation of that passage, is found to be in strict context with the post-tribulation day of the Lord. Therefore, it is critical to understand that Paul's citation initially identifies the last trumpet of the church *rapture* as one that is to be in conjunction with a post-tribulation occasion, and that absolutely no correlation can be found concerning a pre-tribulation sounding.

Fortunately, this is thoroughly verified in the book of Isaiah. Further study of the passage surrounding verse 8 Paul uses in Isaiah 25 reveals that the context concerning the post-tribulation day of the Lord doesn't stop at that juncture, but evidently continues all the way to the end of Isaiah chapter 27 (and beyond). It is in Isaiah 27:12-13 that the persisting harmony of Paul's *rapture* passage with Isaiah's prophecy reverberates another wave of confirmation.

Isaiah 27:12-13
¹²And it shall come to pass in that day, that the LORD shall beat off from the channel of the river un-

*to the stream of Egypt, and **ye shall be gathered**
one by one, O ye children of Israel.*
*[13]And it shall come to pass **in that day**, (context:
the day of the Lord) that **the great trumpet** shall
be blown, and they shall come which were ready to
perish in the land of Assyria, and the outcasts in the
land of Egypt, and shall worship the LORD in the
holy mount at Jerusalem.*

Isaiah's foretelling prophecy reveals that, indeed, a great
trumpet is to be blown on that day along with the gathering
of the elect. Since Paul is clearly pointing the readers of his
rapture passage of I Corinthians 15 to Isaiah's, then the last
trumpet to herald the *rapture* of the church is, in fact, this
particular trumpet blast of Isaiah 27:13 which is, without
doubt, in context with both Isaiah 25:8 (Paul's *rapture*)
and the post-tribulation day of the Lord (Isaiah 24:21-23).
Fortunately, this clear connection between the writings
of Isaiah and Paul concerning the day of the Lord and this
particular trumpet, along with the glorious gathering of the
church was not an exclusive one because it is found in
many other areas of Scripture as well. For example:

Joel 2:1-2
*[1]**Blow ye the trumpet** in Zion, and sound an
alarm in my holy mountain: let all the inhabitants of
the land tremble: for the **day of the LORD** cometh,
for it is nigh at hand;*
*[2]A day of darkness and of gloominess, a day of
clouds and of thick darkness, as the morning spread
upon the mountains: **a great people and a
strong**; there hath not been ever the like, neither
shall be any more after it, even to the years of many
generations.*

Just like Isaiah 27:13, again it is found that a trumpet will be blown on the day of the Lord. Unfortunately, many Biblical scholars have misidentified the "great people and a strong" (described immediately after) as a reference to either some kind of demonic army or locust swarm since they are depicted as rushing through the land and devouring it with fire (vs. 3); fully exempt from the grip of death (vs 8).

What is often overlooked is that first, this particular group of people are indeed...people. This is a clear distinction (vs. 2). Second, they are depicted as protruding some sort of glorious aura "as the morning spread upon the mountains" (vs. 2). This is an indication of a people who would have most likely experienced a glorious transformation from mortality into immortality—explaining their exemption from death—and will be projecting a glory similar to what Joel could only describe as that of a morning sunrise. Furthermore, this particular group will march forward in specific ranks (vs 7) and overtake their enemies *"like a thief"* (vs 9). Paul stated in I Thessalonians 5:2-3 that the day of the Lord will come "like a thief in the night" and with "sudden destruction" which is exactly what is being portrayed here in Joel chapter 2 only that Joel sees a great gathering of people being present at that time as well. However, Paul *also* described a great gathering of people in his I Thessalonians passage who will *also* shine gloriously and be exempt from death—*those of the resurrection and rapture of the church!* This is Joel's "great people and a strong" of verse 2!

Paul also said in I Thessalonians 5:4 that we are "children of the light." Although being a child of the light has very real spiritual connotations, upon comparing I Thessalonians 5 with Joel 2, it is evident that it also has literal implications and speaks of the glorious light of Christ which will physically project from every believer at the glorious transformation of the church on the day of the Lord. Again, Joel could only describe this as a dazzling sunrise consuming the night sky.

The identity of this group is further unveiled in Joel 2:10-11.

Joel 2:10-11
[10]The earth shall quake before them; the heavens shall tremble: the sun and the moon shall be dark, and the stars shall withdraw their shining:
*[11]And the LORD shall utter his voice before **his army: for his camp** is very great: for he is strong that executeth his word: for the day of the LORD is great and very terrible; and who can abide it?*

First, it must be re-emphasized that verse ten sets a clear time frame for this entire event by describing the exact celestial occurrences that Jesus stated will not, in any way, take place until after the great tribulation (Matt. 24:29). It is here, however, that the great and strong people of verse 2 are finally revealed in verse 11 as the *Lord's army and camp.* Just like the prophet Isaiah, Joel again describes a sounding of a trumpet on the post-tribulation day of the Lord (Joel 2:1) where a great group of people are gathered together and found to be operating in the glorious power of the Lord.

In Zephaniah, it is addressed yet again.

Zephaniah 1:14-16,18
*[14]The great **day of the LORD** is near, it is near, and hasteth greatly, even the voice of the day of the LORD: the mighty man shall cry there bitterly.*
*[15]That day is a day of wrath, a day of trouble and distress, a day of wasteness and desolation, **a day***

*of darkness and gloominess, a day of clouds
and thick darkness,*
¹⁶*A day of the trumpet and alarm against the
fenced cities, and against the high towers.*
¹⁸*Neither their silver nor their gold shall be able to
deliver them in the day of the LORD's wrath; but the
whole land shall be devoured by the fire of his jealousy: for he shall make even a speedy riddance of all
them that dwell in the land.*

Again, the day of the Lord is signified by an ominous darkness which will encompass the land but that Zephaniah claims will also be "a day of the trumpet"—just as Isaiah and Joel reveal in their writings. It's important to note that the timing of this particular day-of-the-Lord trumpet sound is reaffirmed as a post-tribulation event in every Old Testament appearance through the repeated use of the celestial markers clearly laid out be Christ in Matthew 24:29.

It's also important to point out here in Zephaniah that the fire of verse 18 is a fire associated with the Lord's jealously. This has an obvious correlation to the great and strong people of Joel 2:2 who are *also* consuming the land with fire—a clear indication that this group (the church, along with the armies of heaven) will be operating in this particular power of the Lord on that day.

-The New Testament-

The great trumpet/day of the Lord/gathering of people connection was not limited to the Old Testament and is also specifically mentioned by Jesus in Matthew 24.

Matthew 24:29
Immediately after the tribulation of those days shall the **sun be darkened,** *and the* **moon shall not give her light,** *and the* **stars shall fall from heaven,** *and the powers of the heavens shall be shaken:*

While this verse has already been mentioned multiple times, again, it needs to be recognized that Jesus describes the exact celestial events that are synonymous with the Old Testament day of the Lord according to the books of Joel, Isaiah, and Zephaniah. Then Jesus continues:

30And then shall appear the sign of the Son of man in heaven: and then shall all the tribes of the earth mourn, and they shall see the Son of man coming in the clouds of heaven with power and great glory.
31And he shall send his angels with a **great sound of a trumpet,** *and they shall* **gather together his elect** *from the four winds, from one end of heaven to the other.*

According to the very words of the Messiah, a great trumpet will sound immediately after the great tribulation on the day of the Lord where the elect of God are to be gathered at that time! This provides a *third* confirmation concerning the timing of Isaiah's trumpet of Isaiah 27:13.

This also weakens the case for those who would claim that even though the great and strong people of Joel 2:2 could possibly be a reference to the present day church; the church was merely caught up prior to the day of the Lord and was returning from heaven with the Lord after the great tribulation. According to Christ, the gathering must occur on the post-tribulation day of the Lord and not prior.

Many have also tried standing on the claim that there are translation discrepancies between the Old Testament Hebrew and the New Testament Greek concerning the word "trumpet" in order to disconnect the last trump of I Corinthians 15:52 from the great trumpet associated with the Old Testament post-tribulation day of the Lord. *Paul's utilization of Isaiah 25:8 in I Corinthians 15:54 clearly overrides this school of thought.* Paul's citation becomes vastly critical one more time since it confirms that the *rapture* of the church is an event strictly limited to the post-tribulation day of the Lord according to Isaiah, which, in turn, *requires the last trumpet of I Corinthians 15 to be a post-tribulation trumpet as well.* This is thoroughly verified, first and most importantly, in Isaiah's passage—where Paul is indisputably getting his *rapture* doctrine from—in which Isaiah confirms Paul's last trumpet sound as that of a post-tribulation trumpet in Isaiah 27:13. This is due to the clear context setting established in Isaiah 24:23.

Alone, Isaiah's post-tribulation day-of-the-Lord trumpet blast is further supported by other Old Testament prophets with additional substantiation found in the New Testament coming from the very words of Jesus Christ. These truths trace a line that begins in I Corinthians 15, walks back through the Old Testament, turns around, re-enters through the gates of the New Testament, and comes to rest at the unavoidable post-tribulation message of Matthew 24 once more.

Though the parallels between Paul's other major *rapture* passage of I Thessalonians 4/5 and Matthew 24 are overwhelming, a disconnection by pre-tribulation theorists is still attempted but is of little use since his other major *rapture* passage, found in I Corinthians, *still ends up at Matthew 24.*

Paul's last trump of I Corinthians 15:52 is in direct reference to the great trumpet that will sound on the post-tribulation day of the Lord where the church will finally be changed at that time.

Marriage of the Lamb

If you have ever found yourself in a discussion about the return of Christ in one form or another, then it's more than likely that you have also run across the phrase: "The Marriage of the Lamb." Seasoned believers usually understand its overall concept to varying degrees, however, almost all conversations I've had concerning this marriage seem to end up brief. It's brought up quickly and then pushed aside to discuss other aspects concerning the end, leading me to believe there is only limited knowledge surrounding this mysterious event.

The first mention of this marriage within the book of Revelation can be found in chapter 19.

Revelation 19:7
*Let us be glad and rejoice, and give honour to him: for **the marriage of the Lamb is come**, and his wife hath made herself ready.*

Again, some within the church are somewhat familiar with this term and what it entails, but for those who aren't, let me quickly summarize it because the key to unlocking the mystery of this marriage is by first obtaining an accurate definition.

First, in envisioning a marriage, we picture a ceremony involving a bride and a bridegroom. Who is that bride in relation to the Lamb's wedding?

I Corinthians 11:2
*For I am jealous over you with godly jealousy: for I have espoused you to one husband, that I may present you as a **chaste virgin to Christ**.*

Ephesians 5:25-27
*²⁵**Husbands, love your wives, even as Christ also loved the church, and gave himself for it;***
²⁶That he might sanctify and cleanse it with the washing of water by the word,
²⁷That he might present it to himself a glorious church, not having spot, or wrinkle, or any such thing; but that it should be holy and without blemish.

The church is that bride. These passages use the example of marriage to describe our role as the collective church. If the church is the bride, then who is the Lamb? John the Baptist made that evident when he saw Jesus coming toward him in the distance—to which he firmly declared to the public:

John 1:29
*...Behold the **Lamb** of God, which taketh away the sin of the world.*

The Lamb is Jesus Christ. Please note the simplicity yet importance of this next statement: If the bride is a *picture* of the church, and the Lamb is a *picture* of Christ, then the marriage of the Lamb is merely a _picture_ of the event or ceremony which will unite Christ with His bride. _That event is none other than the resurrection and rapture of the church!_ This has been long awaited by the elect because it is to be a time of great joy. We will no longer be held under the bondage of the flesh, being made incorruptible in compliance with the Kingdom of God—no more tears and no more sorrow!

Now that an accurate definition has initially been obtained (one that will be proven with Scripture a little later), a return to the original mention of the marriage in Revelation 19 becomes of increasing interest to see if there are any indications of its timing.

First, the beginning of chapter 19 reveals a great gathering of people in heaven giving glory to God because His judgment has finally come upon the "great whore."

Revelation 19:1-2
[1]And after these things I heard a great voice of much people in heaven, saying, Alleluia; Salvation, and glory, and honor, and power, unto the Lord our God:
[2]For true and righteous are his judgments: for **he hath judged the great whore**, which did corrupt the earth with her fornication, and hath avenged the blood of his servants at her hand.

This "great whore" is an obvious reference to the whore of Revelation 17:5...

And upon her forehead was a name written, **MYSTERY, BABYLON THE GREAT**, THE MOTHER OF HARLOTS AND ABOMINATIONS OF THE EARTH.

Quickly summarized, Satan, at the time of the end, will set up the headquarters to his wicked kingdom in a great city of the world. The angel explains to John that the whore with the label "mystery, Babylon the great" upon her forehead is a representation of this city—a city marked by seven hills (Revelation 17:19)—which will ride the power of the Beast system. Of course, the most famous seven-hilled city today is Rome. Of even more interest is a small independent state which is settled right in the heart of Rome known as Vatican City—home to the Roman Catholic Church...but I digress. The point is, the beginning of Revelation 19 depicts the aftermath of this city's destruction from a heavenly aspect, ultimately revealing that *Babylon has now fallen* at this point—a key factor in determining an accurate timeline of events as will soon be addressed.

Continuing on, John then hears the large multitude of voices thundering "as the voice of many waters."

Revelation 19:6-7
⁶And I heard as it were the voice of a great multitude, and as the voice of many waters, and as the voice of mighty thunderings, saying, Alleluia: for the Lord God omnipotent reigneth.
⁷Let us be glad and rejoice, and give honour to him: for, **the marriage of the Lamb is come** *and his wife hath made herself ready.*

Once Babylon had fallen, this same large multitude makes another thunderous unified statement that "the marriage of the Lamb _is_ come." Notice the present tense—*is* come (Authorized King James Version), not *has* come. The Greek manuscript associates with the marriage here strictly in the present tense. The "is" is critical because it tells us that _this is_ the actual time of the marriage and that it has not occurred previously. If it said "has come," some might conjecture that it has already occurred. This is simply not the case.

The conclusion is, chapter 19 reveals a specific order of events that begins with the destruction of "mystery, Babylon the Great," and is then followed by the infamous marriage of the Lamb.

To understand where these two events sit in relation to the time of the end, a passage must be found that broadens our perception a little further. A study of Revelation 13 and 14 does this in the form of an irrefutable chronological timeline of events involving the entire end of the age, beginning with the great tribulation and ending with the battle of Armageddon at the end of chapter 14.

As you can see, the destruction of Babylon is clearly placed after the great tribulation on this timeline. Since the marriage of the Lamb won't take place until after the destruction of Babylon (according to Revelation 19), then it can be quickly concluded that the marriage of the Lamb must occur after the great tribulation as well. Since the marriage is merely a representation of the *rapture,* then the preliminary indication is that the *rapture* of the church must occur *after* the great tribulation.

This is great initial proof of the *rapture's* true end time positioning; however, some still try to place the marriage/*rapture* at the beginning of Daniel's seventieth week to allow for a supposed seven year marriage celebration. Since a marriage certainly comes before a marriage celebration, then why doesn't John place the marriage somewhere back in the twelfth chapter—before the Beast rises— to harmonize with that viewpoint? Was he confused on the timing, or can a parallel be found to reinforce his approach to the order he provided in Revelation 19? To answer this question, what must be first understood is that much of the book of Revelation is repetitive in nature. Most any subject found within Revelation is probably discussed elsewhere in the book, only from a different perspective. That is the thrust of Revelation 13 and 14. These chapters are actually corresponding passages to Revelation 19. I have listed them side by side for comparison.

Revelation 13/14	Revelation 19
Babylon is fallen. (Rev. 14:8)	Babylon is fallen. (Rev. 19:2)
Christ sends his angels to gather the elect. (Rev. 14:15)	**The Marriage of the Lamb is come.** (Rev. 19:7)
Christ sends his angels to gather the wicked. (Rev. 14:19)	Satan's armies gathered at Armageddon. (Rev. 19:19)
Winepress is trodden. (Battle of Armageddon –Rev. 14:20)	Winepress is trodden. (Battle of Armageddon –Rev. 19:15)

The timeline found in Revelation 13 and 14 is a vital study tool because if you find yourself in other areas of Revelation—uncertain of when a particular event will unfold, then simply comparing the terminology that confronts you with this important timeline will quickly get you re-orientated to determining the position of that event in the overall grand scheme. Using this technique, Revelation 19 reveals itself to be the *exact same* timeline found at the end of the Revelation 13/14 timeline, and is simply being re-addressed as further confirmation by the writer. Upon comparing the two passages, everything is identical except for one thing. The only difference found in chapter 19 is this: Instead of stating that the angels are sent to gather the elect like he does in chapter 14, John chose to insert the term "the marriage of the Lamb" in its place. The truth is, he wasn't writing about something new here. Instead, the apostle John was merely describing the *exact same event* of chapter 14—*only figuratively* in chapter 19. This exposes an immensely critical piece of evidence! The gathering of the elect by the angels of Revelation 14—an event clearly set to take place after the great tribulation—*is* the marriage of the Lamb of Revelation 19!

This striking information provides a clear and much-needed scriptural definition for the marriage, undeniably proving that the marriage of the Lamb is simply designed to *figuratively* describe a *literal* post-tribulation gathering of the elect. This truth disconnects the marriage from any pre-tribulation insinuation whatsoever. To infer that the church must be taken out prior to the great tribulation because there needs to be time for a marriage celebration is actually in direct opposition to the Word—made abundantly clear by the previously mentioned truths.

But why does John choose to describe the marriage of the Lamb literally in chapter 14, but figuratively in chapter

19? *It's because this is exactly what Christ does in Matthew 24 when prophesying to His disciples about the end!* First, Jesus begins by describing the gathering from a literal perspective.

> *Matthew 24:30-31*
> *30And then shall appear the sign of the Son of man in heaven: and then shall all the tribes of the earth mourn, and they shall see the Son of man coming in the clouds of heaven with power and great glory.*
> *31And he shall **send his angels** with a great sound of a trumpet, and they shall **gather together his elect** from the four winds, from one end of heaven to the other.*

At the time of the resurrection and *rapture*, Jesus will descend from heaven, but in all actuality, *He will send His angels* to gather His elect while He waits for us in the air. We will then meet Him there as referenced in I Thessalonians 4:17—"to meet the Lord in the air." Then, in the very next chapter, Jesus begins speaking figuratively by way of parable about 5 out of 10 worthy virgins *meeting a Bridegroom for a marriage*. Again, the Bridegroom is a clear representation of *Jesus Christ*—the Lamb slain since the foundation of the world (Rev. 13:8)—and the virgins are another reference to the *church* (2 Cor. 11:2). The truth is, the "marriage of the Lamb" concept—utilized in the book of Revelation—*actually originated with this parable spoken of by Christ*. It was merely a type or picture that Christ used to help us understand the mysteries concerning the gathering of the elect—a gathering that is to occur immediately after the great tribulation according to the statement He had made just moments earlier in the chapter. Once more, in the book of Matthew, the marriage parable is found to be *figuratively* describing a *literal* post-tribulation gathering of the elect and is merely the same marriage of the Lamb that John references in Revelation 19. Curiously, pre-tribulation believers associate the parable of the 10 virgins with the pre-tribulation *rapture* of the church, but completely ignore the post-tribulation context that is clearly in operation.

Confusion reigns over this subject because most think there has to be an allotted amount of time for an actual marriage celebration in heaven, and the only way that could be feasible is if we are taken out sometime prior to His actual Second Coming. How could Christ collect His church after the great tribulation, partake in a wedding celebration, and hand out rewards to His servants all while coming down from heaven to wage war at the battle of Armageddon? The answer is that the marriage of the Lamb is *strictly figurative* and was merely a symbol or aid used by Christ and the apostle John to help us fully understand the mysteries of the *rapture* and of the coming Kingdom. In truth, Christ will descend with all power and glory with His angels after the great tribulation. When this occurs, the *figurative* marriage (resurrection/*rapture*) will take place. The righteous, being separated from the wicked, will ultimately enter into the blessings of the millennial kingdom (celebration), while the wicked are destroyed at the battle of Armageddon and sent into everlasting destruction.

I regard the marriage study to be one of *the* most powerful tools in exposing the pre-tribulation *rapture* theory as false doctrine, and is even more powerful in proving a post-tribulation gathering of the church. However, I have come to quickly realize in my time divulging this subject that while the banner of truth, backed by proof, is waved freely for all to see, it's still your choice to either receive it or forfeit it.

I earnestly pray that you receive it right now for your spiritual benefit, and for the benefit of the church. In the mighty Name of Jesus. Amen.

Resurrection
of the Dead

As Christians, the very core of our salvation depends on whether we believe a resurrection from death back to life is even plausible.

Romans 10:9
*That if thou shalt confess with thy mouth the Lord Jesus, and **shalt believe in thine heart that God hath raised him from the dead**, thou shalt be saved.*

If Christ died, remained in His grave, and never conquered death, then our faith is completely invalid. It is essential that we believe in the resurrection of Christ. There were some believers in the early church who were making claims that a resurrection from death back to life was impossible. Paul was quick to stomp this rumor out by telling the church that if they didn't believe it possible, then they were still in their sins and lost forever—their hope and faith in Christ being worthless in value.

The good news, for those of us who *do* believe that Christ was raised from the dead, is we are rested and assured that the future resurrection of believers, also taught by Christ, will occur at its appointed time. His resurrection validates the one He spoke of to come in the near future! It proves who He said He was (and is, and is to come), and gives us hope of eternal life in Jesus, and a resurrection into a new body at the time of the end!

Paul's letter to the Corinthian church offers valuable insight into the timing of this coming resurrection, which ultimately guides us into truth about the *rapture* timing.

I Corinthians 15:20-23
20But now is Christ risen from the dead, and become the first fruits of them that slept.
21For since by man came death, by man came also the resurrection of the dead.
22For as in Adam all die, even so in Christ shall all be made alive.
23But every man in his own order: Christ the firstfruits; afterward they that are Christ's at his coming.

Notice that he lists only *two* resurrections: Christ's resurrection, and the resurrection of those "that are Christ's at His coming." Christ's resurrection took place almost 2000 years ago when He rose from the dead after three days in a rich man's tomb. (Hallelujah!) Paul aptly labeled this pivotal event the "first fruits" resurrection. Interestingly enough, the day Jesus rose, is the same day that the Jewish celebration known as the feast of first fruits took place—but that's another book altogether! My point is to display how perfect and operational God's plan really is.

According to Paul, the next resurrection to occur will be those "that are Christ's at His coming." Fortunately, he speaks of other events that will come about at that same time, giving us important insight into the timing.

I Corinthians 15:24
Then cometh the end, when shall have delivered up the kingdom to God, even the Father; when he shall have put down all rule and all authority and power.

This particular resurrection is to occur at the same time that Christ comes back to set up His *millennial kingdom*. Since the Bible is steadfast in validating its positions in other areas, there's usually a parallel passage to help solidify its truth. In relation to I Corinthians 15:24, Revelation 20 is that passage. Here is the first parallel:

Revelation 20:1-3
¹And I saw an angel come down from heaven, having the key of the bottomless pit and a great chain in his hand.
²And he laid hold on the dragon, that old serpent, which is the Devil, and Satan, and bound him a thousand years,
³And cast him into the bottomless pit, and shut him up, and set a seal upon him, that he should deceive the nations no more, till the thousand years should be fulfilled: and after that he must be loosed a little season.

When Christ returns, He will come to put down all rule and authority on earth (I Cor. 15:24). This is ultimately accomplished by binding Satan for the duration of Christ's 1000 year reign.

The second parallel is found in verses 4-6...

Revelation 20:4-5

⁴*And I saw thrones, and they sat upon them, and judgment was given unto them: and I saw the souls of them that were beheaded for the witness of Jesus, and for the word of God, and which had not worshipped the beast, neither his image, neither had received his mark upon their foreheads, or in their hands; and they lived and reigned with Christ a thousand years.*

⁵*But the rest of the dead lived not again until the thousand years were finished.* **This is the first resurrection.**

Verse 5 tends to be a little confusing at first because it seems to be connecting the first resurrection with the "rest of the dead" who won't live again until the thousand years are completed. However, John is actually referring to the contents of verse 4 when he mentions the first resurrection. The first sentence of verse 5 is actually a continued thought beyond the context provided in verse 4. How is the conclusion made? Verse 6 provides the evidence.

⁶**Blessed and holy is he that hath part in the first resurrection:** *on such the second death hath no power, but they shall be priests of God and of Christ, and shall* **reign with him a thousand years.**

John reveals that the participants of the first resurrection are actually to be the ones to rule and reign with Christ *throughout* the entire 1000 year course, thus placing the first resurrection at the beginning of the millennial kingdom and not at the end with the rest of the dead.

Furthermore, the participants of the first resurrection

were also described as those who did not worship the Beast, neither his image, neither did they take the mark of the Beast (Revelation 20:4). Of course, it is widely accepted that these events are to occur throughout the great tribulation, ultimately revealing that the partakers of the first resurrection would have had to suffer through the entire course of the great tribulation before participating in it. This information places the first resurrection of Revelation 20 after the great tribulation as well, *ultimately requiring it to be a strict post-tribulation/pre-millennial event.*

John was also careful to note that it was the _first_ resurrection. He didn't claim that it was "part B" of a previous secret resurrection, but that it was the *first* (following Christ's resurrection). Again, it is the resurrection of those "that are Christ's at His coming" (the post-tribulation/pre-millennial coming) and is found to be the second parallel to I Corinthians 15 (vs. 23).

When this evidence is brought to light, pre-tribulation theorists begin speculating that their secret *rapture* of the living will still take place prior to this particular resurrection. But is this scenario a scriptural possibility?

I Thessalonians 4:16-17
16For the Lord himself shall descend from heaven with a shout, with the voice of the archangel, and with the trump of God: **and the dead in Christ shall rise first:**

According to this passage, the resurrection of the dead in Christ must rise first...

17Then we which are alive and remain shall be caught up together with them in the clouds, to meet the Lord in the air: and so shall we ever be with the Lord.

...*then* the *rapture* takes place; not vice versa! This pre-arranges the order of the resurrection and the *rapture*, revealing that the *rapture* cannot occur prior to the resurrection of the dead. Again:

I Thessalonians 4:15
For this we say unto you by the word of the Lord, that we which are alive and remain unto the coming of the Lord shall not **prevent** *them which are asleep.*

The Greek word used for prevent is <u>*phthano*</u>. It means to become before or precede. Again, the *rapture* cannot *precede* or *come before* the resurrection. The *rapture* verses of I Corinthians 15 concur:

I Corinthians 15:51-53
[51]Behold, I shew you a mystery; We shall not all sleep, but we shall all be changed,
[52]In a moment, in the twinkling of an eye, at the last trump: for the trumpet shall sound, **and the dead shall be raised incorruptible**, *and* **we shall be changed**.

There's the order again: The dead are raised first. Then, those who are alive and remain shall be changed. And once more:

[53]For this corruptible must put on incorruption, and this mortal must put on immortality.

82

Without a doubt, the Bible clearly teaches that the *rapture* must take place after the resurrection.

If any attempt is made to insert a secret resurrection with an attached secret *rapture* so as to maintain a particular view, then you will have just entangled yourself in a circular web because Paul stated very clearly in I Corinthians 15:23 that there is only *one more resurrection coming*, and it is to transpire when Christ returns to set up His millennial kingdom after the great tribulation. Any theories that step outside of Paul's writing have just become speculation. Mark Twain said it best: *"There are two times in a man's life when he should not speculate: when he can't afford it, and when he can."* The point is, you should never speculate! If you never get off the merry-go-round, then you will just become increasingly confused about where you stand.

With this information in the storage banks, the timing of the church *rapture* is now cemented by Paul's arrangement of I Corinthians 15. Adhering to the exact same format offered to the Thessalonians, he begins by first describing the post-tribulation resurrection of those "that are Christ's at His coming." He then takes the opportunity, starting in verse 35 and all the way to the first mention of the *rapture* in verse 51, to describe how that *particular resurrection* will unfold. Immediately after the description of that *particular post-tribulation resurrection*, he begins explaining the mystery of the *rapture* involving the church. Paul specifically inserted the explanation *here* because he wanted to keep everything in chronological order! The *rapture* of the church will not occur until *after* the resurrection of those "who are Christ's at His coming" which, in itself, won't take place until Christ returns to set up His millennial kingdom.

Once again, this places the *rapture* of the church after the great tribulation at the genesis of the Messiah's millennial rule and reign.

The Operation
of Revelation

If throughout the previous chapters, you've been keeping a record of my references to the church *rapture* in
relation to the book of Revelation, you may have noticed that I've now given you, what seems like, five different
church gatherings listed in five different areas of Revelation. The first was addressed in the first chapter in relation
to the sixth seal of Revelation 6. The second correlation
was to the last trumpet of Revelation 11. Two more references to the church *rapture* were made in conjunction with
Revelation 14:14-16 and Revelation 19:7—both discussed in
relation to the marriage of the Lamb. Lastly, one was made
at the first resurrection of Revelation 20 in the previous
chapter. How can this be a possibility if there really is only
one church *rapture* coming in the near future? To answer
this question correctly, a study of how the book of Revelation operates is necessary in order to understand how the
Author has constructed its layout. When taking on this
task, all we can do is find the facts, apply them, steer clear
of any speculation, and in time let God fill in the blanks.

There are a million different charts, graphs, fold-outs, and pop-ups (that would be unique!) associated with Revelation floating around these days, carrying an array of diverse ideas, theories, and notions. By the time you sort through them all, you don't know if you're coming or going! Most of them don't make much sense because they are carrying pre-conceived ideas and completely ignore what is actually trying to be conveyed. This chapter is designed to simply introduce you to Revelation's true intent, and guide you through the front doors of Revelation chronology. I'm confident that once it has taken root, more exciting details will naturally spring forward when studying on your own.

-The Trumpets-

Let's begin with the trumpets. Because the seven trumpets are listed after the unveiling of the seventh seal, most assume that this is where they begin. A closer look reveals to the contrary. A study of the seven trumpets unlocks many important details that actually disqualify them from occurring after the seals. The most noticeable evidence manifests at the fifth trumpet. First, this particular trumpet blast opens a bottomless pit by a "star" with a key. Stars are symbolic for angels here, so an angel sounds the fifth trumpet and another angel falls from heaven, is given a key to the bottomless pit, and unlocks it. Once unlocked, a beast ascends out of the abyss.

Revelation 17:8
The beast that thou sawest was, and is not; **and shall ascend out of the bottomless pit**, *and go into perdition:*

Revelation 11:7
And when they shall have finished their testimony,
the beast that ascendeth out of the bottomless
pit *shall make war against them, and shall over-*
come them, and kill them.

This beast is ultimately a reference to the end time Antichrist. It is this particular Beast who will arise out of the bottomless pit, claim sole power of the world during the great tribulation, and wage war against the saints.

Revelation 13:5,7
5And there was given unto him a mouth speaking
great things and blasphemies; and power was given
unto him to continue **forty and two months.**
(great tribulation)
7And it was given unto him to make **war with the**
saints, *and to overcome them: and power was giv-*
en him over all kindreds, and tongues, and nations.

Therefore, it can be concluded, with much ease, that the great tribulation *cannot even begin* until the fifth trumpet sound—the obvious reason being that this particular Beast cannot come out of his pit nor can the great tribulation begin until this bottomless pit is, at least, unlocked. Simply put: no Beast equals no great tribulation! Again, since the Bible is clear that the Beast will not be unlocked from his domain until the fifth trumpet, it means the great tribulation cannot even begin until the fifth trumpet is sounded. This is a simple yet severely overlooked and critical piece of information as I will soon reveal.

At the sixth trumpet blast, a devastating war takes place that ultimately annihilates a third of mankind. Moving quickly away from that dismal reality, we come to the seventh trumpet sound which reveals that "The kingdoms of the world are become the kingdoms of Lord, and of His Christ," the dead are judged, rewards are given to His servants, and God's "wrath is come." From a previous chapter, we've learned that the events of the seventh trumpet happen *after* the great tribulation. Therefore, the overall conclusion that can be made is that, in relation to all seven trumpets, the time of great tribulation spoken of by Christ and the prophets must occur at the *fifth and sixth trumpet blasts*. This is the very reason why the fifth trumpet is labeled the first woe!

-Christ Confirms-

Solid confirmation of the fifth trumpet/great tribulation connection can be found in Matthew 24. There, Christ is informing His disciples of how the days will be shortened during the great tribulation period.

Matthew 24:21-22
[21]For then shall be **great tribulation***, such as was not since the beginning of the world to this time, no, nor ever shall be.*
*[22]**And except those days should be shortened***, *there should no flesh be saved:*

The significance is, if you go back to the fourth trumpet (which is just prior to the unlocking of the bottomless pit and the great tribulation period), a description of shortened days is positioned perfectly—just as Christ foretells in Matthew 24.

Revelation 8:12
And the fourth angel sounded, and the third part of
the sun was smitten, and the third part of the moon,
and the third part of the stars; so as the third part of
them was darkened, and **the day shone not for a**
third part of it, and the night likewise.

A third of day and a third of night is blotted out, leaving a third of a 24 hour period remaining. When the fourth trumpet sounds, a full day as we know it now will only constitute eight hours, leaving a meager four hours of daylight. This brings to light what was being referenced in Amos 8:

And it shall come to pass in that day, saith the Lord
GOD, that I will cause the **sun to go down at**
noon, *and I will darken the earth in the clear day:*

The sun will come up in the morning and set at noontime. Why does God decide to tinker with time at this moment? Christ answers that question:

Matthew 24:22
...for the elect's sake those days shall be shortened.

First, for those who find themselves in the great tribulation period, they will witness signs in the skies that are unprecedented in history which will be a signal to the true elect that Christ is about to return (Luke 21:25). Those who are watching will understand what's going on in the heavens. Second, the war against the saints will be so brutal during that period that if God didn't literally shorten time, there would be no one left to collect when Christ actually returns. That paints a pretty ugly picture, but it's truth nonetheless.

I must deviate from the overall subject for a quick moment and state that if you actually find yourself in the middle of this turmoil someday, there is a silver lining to this very dark cloud. If the fourth trumpet is meant to be taken literally (and I believe that it is), and the great tribulation is indeed shortened by two thirds to a third of the time, then what we get is the short math section of this book. If we multiply .33 x 1260 we get 415.8—which isn't completely accurate. If we change the values to hours, we get a much more accurate assessment.

First, $1/3^{rd}$ of a 24 hour period is 8 hours. How many hours are in 1260 days if one day constitutes 8 hours?

$$1260 \times 8 = 10,080 \text{ hours.}$$

To find out how many normal 24 hour days as we know it now could be extracted from 10,080 hours, simply take 10,080 hours and divide it by 24.

$$10,080 \text{hrs} / 24 \text{ hrs} = 420 \text{ days.}$$

By this calculation, it's revealed that the great tribulation really only lasts *a little over a year*. It will *still be* 1260 days, only these particular "days" will literally be shortened just as Christ prophesied in Matthew 24. This shortened period will certainly be a little ray of hope for those under the hammer of the Beast, and is designed solely for the protection of the believers who must endure the great tribulation.

But in relation to the subject of this chapter, the fourth trumpet becomes an excellent source of affirmation that the great tribulation begins at the fifth trumpet because of how it lines up with Christ's description concerning that same time period in Matthew 24 so perfectly.

While still on the subject of shortened days, I must make mention at this juncture about the pre-wrath position, which is essentially a carbon copy of the post-tribulation view with emphasis on a shortened great tribulation period that is cut off by the day of the Lord. I believe this position to be correct—as long as it's explained by the fourth trumpet. However, to state that the great tribulation will be cut off before the 1260 days have fulfilled their course would contradict Scripture because it's clear that the great tribulation is indeed 1260 days in length. How then, can you fulfill the 1260 days of the great tribulation but still shorten its length? The answer is: *in its days.* It is the fourth trumpet that unlocks this mystery by revealing that the individual days are going to be shortened. This allows for a cut-off of the great tribulation period while still adhering to the prophecy concerning the 1260 day length.

-The seals-

Now that we've taken a look at the trumpets, a study of the seals is needed to see how they function in relation. Many suppose that when the first seal is broken, it begins a series of events that continues in chronological order throughout the entire book of Revelation until the battle of Armageddon. Since I have previously established that the sixth seal contains celestial events that are to occur immediately *after* the great tribulation (according to Christ in Matthew 24:29), then why do we come across these post-tribulation components so quickly? Shouldn't this timeframe have been found closer to Christ's descent from heaven on a white horse, found towards the end of the book? Why is it listed at the beginning of John's revelation of future events?

What must be considered first is that if the entire book

is actually in chronological order from beginning to end, it would mean that all seven trumpets are to occur after the great tribulation because of the position of the post-tribulation sixth seal. However, since I have now shown, with much proof, that the fifth and sixth trumpet sounds occur *within* the great tribulation—not after, it's actually impossible for the seven trumpets to occur after the post-tribulation sixth seal. *The fifth trumpet throws a monkey wrench into the chronological gears.* Again, taking into consideration that the sixth <u>seal</u> occurs immediately *after* the great tribulation (due to its clear relationship with Matthew 24:29), and since the fifth trumpet is the necessary catalyst needed for the great tribulation period to *begin*, we have to come to the conclusion that taking a linear approach to the seals and trumpets would actually reverse time—an impossibility when determining a timeline of events. Therefore, even though the fifth and sixth great-tribulation trumpets are listed after the seven seals, they actually must be sounded *prior to* the opening of the post-tribulation sixth seal somehow. So the question immediately becomes: How can that be a possibility? The answer is: *The trumpets are coinciding with the seals and are occurring simultaneously.* The trumpets' function is to explain contents of the seals, only in greater detail or from an alternate perspective and that the seventh (last) trumpet is actually overlapping the sixth seal. Both the sixth seal and seventh trumpet are describing the same *rapture* event, only from different perspectives. When you come to this realization and begin to investigate them both further, you immediately begin to observe other evident similarities beyond the gathering of the church.

The 6th Seal	The 7th Trumpet
...and, lo, there was a **great earthquake**;... (Rev. 6:12)	...and there were lightnings, and voices, and thunderings, and an **earthquake**... (Rev. 11:19)
For the great day of his **wrath is come;** (Rev. 6:17)	And the nations were angry, and thy **wrath is come,** (Rev. 11:18)

As you can see, both contain an earthquake and both reveal that God's "wrath is come." This is further confirmation of simultaneous occurrence.

This brings forward the true nature of the seven seals and the seven trumpets, revealing their actual functionality and relationship to one another. In truth, Revelation is setup much like a PowerPoint presentation. For those of us who have suffered through endless hours of business meetings, you know that these presentations usually begin with a major overview of the material that will be addressed throughout the course of the meeting. *This is the job of the seven seals.* The seven seals are simply an entire overview of the end—a rough outline expressing only the most major points of all the events that are to unfold at the end of this current age. The first seal is essentially the beginning to all of the end time events that are to unfold and concludes at the seventh seal with the *millennial reign of Christ.* This illuminates the very reason for such a quickly arriving post-tribulation description at the sixth seal. This truth also helps to unlock the mystery of the seventh seal which reveals a silence in heaven. The reason there's a silence is because *no one is there!* When Christ unlooses the seventh seal, the inhabitants of heaven will follow the descending

Messiah and pour out onto earth to come wage war against the wicked at the battle of Armageddon. This will leave heaven totally empty and in complete silence; it's the end all of end all! Of course, it's more than sheer coincidence that a large gathering of saints occurs right before this seal is broken because it's simply confirming what Paul was trying to convey to the Thessalonians: *The church will be caught up on the post-tribulation day of the Lord.*

Once all the major points have been established in a PowerPoint presentation, the speaker returns to each major point and begins to elaborate on each one in further detail, offering a more in depth analysis. *This is the job of the trumpets.* While many are busy advocating that the seven trumpets can only occur upon the unloosing of the seventh seal, again, this is scripturally impossible since the seventh seal occurs *after* the great tribulation yet the great tribulation, from the perspective of the trumpets, *begins* at the fifth trumpet.

Furthermore, a post-seventh-seal sounding of the seven trumpets would make it extremely difficult to explain the reason for a curious retraction from a complete black out of the sun, depicted at the sixth seal, back to the sun only being smitten for a third part of the day at the fourth trumpet. Such reversal is contradictory to the essence of Revelation's nature since the end is only to *increase* in alarming intensity and not vice versa. This creates a legitimate problem for those who hold to the seventh seal/seven trumpets connection. The remedy? Again, the seals and trumpets are actually to occur simultaneously and that the fourth trumpet, when bunk-bedded over the seven seals, is positioned prior to the total darkening of the sun that is to take place at the sixth seal.

I believe the overall confusion as to where to position the trumpets stems from the fact that the seventh seal is separated from Revelation 7 and is placed in chapter 8 where the seven trumpets are first mentioned. This makes it deceivingly easy to attach the two together as one unified event. What must be clearly understood is that chapter and verse division didn't originate with the apostle John, nor did it originate with any other author given the huge responsibility of penning God's Word. While John frantically wrote down the vision revealed to him in his revelation, his last concern would have been to divide it into chapters and assign verses; it wouldn't have been included with the original inspired Word. If you were to be fortunate enough to hold the original copy of John's Revelation, it would appear as a book or a novel (and probably looked like the handwriting from a doctor's prescription because of the intensity of the moment!).

It wasn't till many centuries later that Scholars would finally assign chapters and verses as an indexing service that we are now so familiar with, but would have been undoubtedly subject to personal interpretation. While Scripture is the inspired and Holy Word of God, it must be emphasized that numerical chapter and verse division is not. When Christ read from the book of Isaiah in the second Jewish temple, He would have held a copy void of chapter and verse division. It would have been formatted more like a book with paragraphs.

Here is a quote from Wikipedia.com concerning the division of the New Testament:

"Unlike the Hebrew of the Old Testament, the structure of the Greek language makes it highly susceptible to being broken up into divisions that would be syntactically inappropriate and even contrary to the sense of the passage. Inexact apportionment of the Greek into verses therefore could easily have ob-

scured the intent, relation, emphasis and force of the words themselves, and thus elicited the most strenuous objections of theologians"

Determining the relationship between the seventh seal and the seven trumpets strictly from a neutral perspective reveals that *there is no direct relationship,* and when taking into account all of the other valuable truths previously laid out, it is revealed that the seven angels holding the seven trumpets are to be interpreted as an entirely separate event—unique from the unloosing of the seventh seal. However, the fact that they appear together in the same chapter paints a false picture that they're interdependent and, in the minds of many, are subconsciously connected together.

Here's an exercise: Read through the seventh seal again only this time imagine it's the last verse of chapter 7 while placing chapter 8 verse 2 in the place of the seventh seal's old address. Here's what it would look like:

Revelation 7

[16]They shall hunger no more, neither thirst any more; neither shall the sun light on them, nor any heat.

[17]For the Lamb which is in the midst of the throne shall feed them, and shall lead them unto living fountains of waters: and God shall wipe away all tears from their eyes.

"18" *And when he had opened the seventh seal, there was silence in heaven about the space of half an hour.*

"Revelation 8:1"

And I saw the seven angels which stood before God; and to them were given seven trumpets.

While I'm not advocating a mandatory verse relocation program, did you notice that the whole perspective of the seven trumpets immediately changes? The division between the seventh seal and the seven trumpets becomes exponentially clear at this point. I'm well aware that this is controversial ground, so for those of you who are uncomfortable with this notion, I implore you to simply read the passage again—only *without* the persuasion of chapter and verse division (which was my whole point to begin with) and you too will clearly see that there are no legitimate ties between the seventh seal and the seven trumpets. If not keenly aware, the seventh seal could be (and is) easily mistaken for the trumpets' container because of its curious placement in chapter 8, and is the major reason why I believe so many people automatically make this assumption.

As always, parallels can be found in the Old Testament, verifying that the trumpets are indeed intertwined with the seals and that they don't actually occur after the unloosing of the seventh seal. The most remarkable parallel is found in Zephaniah.

Zephaniah 1:14-16
*14The great **day of the LORD** is near, it is near, and hasteth greatly, even the voice of the day of the LORD: the mighty man shall cry there bitterly.*
*15That day is a **day of wrath**, a day of trouble and distress, a day of wasteness and desolation, a day of darkness and gloominess, a day of clouds and thick darkness,*
*16A **day of the trumpet** and alarm against the fenced cities, and against the high towers.*

Zephaniah, in his vision from God, makes a statement that the day of the Lord—a day clearly depicted at the sixth seal in Revelation—is also a day of the trumpet. Which trumpet is being spoken of here? The major clue is that it is a *trumpet associated with God's wrath*. There's only one trumpet in the book of Revelation that offers a description adequate enough to be that candidate...

> *Revelation 11:15,18*
> *And the seventh angel sounded;... (the last trumpet)*
> *...And the nations were angry, and thy **wrath is come,***

It's the seventh and final trumpet of Revelation 11! While pre-tribulation advocates attempt to disconnect the seven trumpets of Revelation from the Old Testament post-tribulation day-of-the-Lord "shofar" trumpet based on the argument that there are translation discrepancies between the Old Testament Hebrew and the New Testament Greek concerning the word "trumpet," the fact that Zephaniah's trumpet and Revelation's last trumpet are both specifically describing the final unleashing of God's wrath on the world scene supersedes this claim. This makes it quite apparent that the final trumpet of Revelation *is* Zephaniah's trumpet. Since Zephaniah also claims that this wrath-filled trumpet will not occur until the day of the Lord, then this places the seventh trumpet of Revelation at the sixth seal day-of-the-Lord event which, in turn, *requires* all six previous trumpet blasts to be sounded prior to the sixth seal as well. If all seven trumpets were not to occur until after the unloosing of the seventh seal, then a contradiction of Scripture would have to be considered here.

This makes Zephaniah's passage an extremely powerful one because not only does it confirm that the sixth seal day-of-the-Lord event and the seventh and final trumpet blast of Revelation occur on the same day, this fact therefore notifies any attentive reader that the seven trumpets of Revelation can't actually sound after the seven seals. Instead, they are to simultaneously unfold together *with* the seals, ultimately proving that the seven trumpets are not contingent upon the opening of the seventh seal.

Moreover, the strength of Zephaniah's passage continues to resonate into Paul's letters because Paul takes the opportunity to describe the *rapture* of the church from the perspective of the day of the Lord in his letter to the Thessalonians, but to the Corinthians, from the perspective of the last trumpet because like Zephaniah, he too understood that both would occur on the same day.

The ripple effect continued into John's writings as well because just as Paul spoke of the *rapture* more than once and from two different perspectives, John also, in the very same manner, offers up a description at the sixth seal from the perspective of the day of the Lord, later, offering up the same description only from the perspective of the last trumpet.

-The Third and Fourth Perspectives-

This overlapping and double view approach was not uncommon throughout John's writing of Revelation. His method was to quickly set a timeline and then return to it immediately afterward to describe certain aspects of that timeline in greater detail or from a different perspective. In fact, he immediately repeated this very process once he had concluded with the seals and trumpets. To understand this concept, however, you must ask yourself these questions: Why, after the seals and trumpets, is there yet another description of the Beast ascending and waging war against the saints during the 42 month great tribulation period (Rev. 13) if that period has already been clearly addressed at the fifth trumpet, and why is there a description concerning the battle of Armageddon at the end of Revelation 14 (vs. 20) if that battle is also described in full detail once more at the end of the book (Rev. 19)? The answer is that Revelation 12-14, once again, reverses gears and readdresses some of the contents and copies the function of the seals by describing, in chronological order, end time events that are to unfold from a *third* perspective, concluding once again with the *battle of Armageddon* at the end of Revelation 14. Then, like the trumpets' relationship to the seals, Revelation 15-19 simply begins explaining certain events on the Revelation 12-14 timeline, only in greater detail.

For instance, in Revelation 14:8 (the original timeline), we learn that "Babylon is fallen, is fallen." Further along in Revelation 18:2 (original timeline readdressed), we read that "Babylon the great is fallen, is fallen." Since we are also told that once Babylon has fallen, it "shall be found no more at all" (Revelation 18:21), and "her smoke rose up forever and ever" (Revelation 19:3), it is to be recognized that Babylon's destruction can't happen twice and that the two verses are actually describing the same destruction, only from two different perspectives. Revelation 14:8 initially speaks of Babylon's fall, while Revelation 18 describes its destruction in greater detail.

Once more, this double view approach occurs with Christ coming to "tread the winepress of the fierceness and wrath of Almighty God." This is first found in Revelation 14:20 (original timeline) and then in Revelation 19:15 (original timeline readdressed).

Fortunately, the church gathering was not exempt from this double perspective. As revealed in a previous chapter, it's listed first in Revelation 14:14-16 (the original timeline), and secondarily, in Revelation 19:7 as the marriage of the Lamb (original timeline readdressed).

The fact that John recycles this format immediately after the seals and trumpets only further verifies that the seven trumpets don't actually occur after the seals and are, in fact, coinciding—designed solely to describe the seals from an alternate perspective.

-The Fifth Perspective-

After describing the battle of Armageddon in vivid detail throughout Revelation 19, John begins Revelation 20 with a depiction of an angel coming down from heaven with the keys to the bottomless pit. Consequently, Satan is finally bound and locked up for a duration of 1000 years; a seal is placed on him so that he "should deceive the nations no more." Then, in Revelation 20:4, John sees "thrones, and they that sat upon them, and judgment was given unto them," followed by a vision of souls who were "beheaded for the witness of Jesus" and "which had not worshipped the Beast" during the great tribulation period. John specifically labels this group of souls to be of the "first resurrection." At first, the indication is that this is exactly where the "first resurrection" event is listed to take place (after the battle of Armageddon). However, a parallel can be found in Matthew 19 which sets the precise timing of this particular resurrection.

> Matthew 19:28
> And Jesus said unto them, (His disciples) Verily I say unto you, That ye which have followed me, in the regeneration (resurrection) when the Son of man shall sit in the throne of his glory, ye also shall sit upon twelve thrones, judging the twelve tribes of Israel.

First, even though John doesn't mention the number of thrones in Revelation 20:4, according to Christ, there are actually to be at least twelve of them, specifically set aside for the Twelve Disciples who will be positioned in elevated nobility next to Christ. They will be given the unique responsibility of judging the twelve tribes of Israel only once the battle of Armageddon has concluded and only once Christ has been seated on His throne of glory in Jerusalem. The "regeneration" Christ mentions is, in fact, the same "first resurrection" that John describes in Revelation 20:5 but that Christ clearly reveals to be as the *first* event to unfold on the day that He is crowned King of kings. This confirms that the "first resurrection" would have actually occurred immediately before the Messiah finally lays rightful claim to His throne and the Disciples likewise.

Taking into account this parallel, when John wrote "this is the first resurrection" in Revelation 20:5, he wasn't indicating that this is precisely when it occurs, but more specifically—these are those who had already participated in the first resurrection event and are now in glorified bodies. The intent of Revelation 20:1-6 was to merely provide John with a quick snapshot of the scene that will encompass Christ's throne of glory in Jerusalem immediately after the battle of Armageddon. The glorified souls he saw enveloped around His throne would have been resurrected into their new bodies at the Second Coming of Christ, saving the church from the day-of-the-Lord wrath that is to be issued out on that same day at the great battle of Armageddon. Once the battle has concluded, the souls of the first resurrection will have already experienced their glorified bodies for a short time, and will then stand before the Son of man (described in Rev. 7:9 and Luke 21:36) as Jesus begins the sheep/goat judgment of the nations on that same day (Matt. 25:32). This is what John sees in Revelation 20:4-6.

-The Big Picture-

All of the information of this chapter, considered in its entirety, provides an accurate overall picture of how the whole book of Revelation is actually constructed, revealing that the same major end time timeline of events is actually described from *four different perspectives*, with an additional "snapshot perspective" provided in Revelation 20 of what is seen around Christ's throne of glory after the battle of Armageddon. Simply put:

- The seven seals initially lay out only the most major points that are to unfold at the entire end of this age, ending with the battle of Armageddon at the seventh seal.
- The seven trumpets describe the seals from a second perspective, ending with the battle of Armageddon.
- Revelation 12-14 describes the seals and the trumpets from a third perspective, ending with the battle of Armageddon.
- Revelation 15-19 describes the end of the Revelation 12-14 timeline only in greater detail and again ends with the battle of Armageddon.
- Revelation 20-22 are events that John witnesses after the battle of Armageddon, centered around Christ's throne of glory.

This quickly illuminates the reason for the five unique church-gathering descriptions found throughout Revelation and are listed on the next page.

The Church *Rapture* Throughout Revelation	
The Seals..Revelation 7:9	
The Trumpets.....................................Revelation 11:15-18	
Revelation 12-14...............................Revelation 14:14-16	
Revelation 15-19..................................Revelation 19:7	
Revelation 20-22................................Revelation 20:4-6	

While the pre-tribulation *rapture* position can only provide one area of seeming scriptural reference in Revelation
4 and 5 in defense of its theory (even then, it's drenched in
symbolism and can't be interpreted literally), this truly remarkable display of reoccurring literal descriptions makes
it extremely difficult to disregard John's actual vision concerning the gathering of the church. The choice is infinitely
clear in this writer's opinion.

Revelation is certainly a mysterious book, but it's not
completely out in left field as some portray. A fortitudinous
approach will reveal many exciting details that will get you
on the path of understanding—*if you keep your own ideas
at arm's length.* A patient and humble heart is the key!

Of course, I couldn't resist in providing my own reference chart, of which, can be found on the following pages.
For the sake of simplicity, I've limited its content to the beginning of the great tribulation onward, but it's still extremely powerful in exposing not only the true function of
Revelation as a whole (since each major end time theme
comes into precise alignment in this configuration), but it
also beautifully showcases the unavoidable reoccurring
message of a post-tribulation *rapture* of the church.

The Operation of Revelation

Revelation 20-22

Rev 20:4-5 1st Resurrection	Rev 20:6 1000 Year Reign of Christ
	Rev 20:3 Satan is Bound

Revelation 15-19

1-4 Vials	Kingdom Full of Darkness 5-7 Vials	Rev 19:7 Marriage of the Lamb	Rev 19:15-21 Winepress is Trodden
		7th Vial Babylon Falls	

Revelation 12-14

Rev 13:1 Beast Rises	Rev 13:5-7 Beast Wars Against Saints 42 Months	Rev 14:14-16 Son of Man on a Cloud Reaps Harvest	Rev 14:19-20 Winepress is Trodden
	Rev 14:1 144,000 in Heaven	Rev 14:8 Babylon Falls	

Revelation 10-11 Parenthetical

2 Witnesses Prophecy 1260 Days	2 Witnesses Caught up + to Heaven

			Earthquake

5th Trumpet	**6th Trumpet**	**7th Trumpet**	
Beast Ascends out of Bottomless Pit	1/3rd of Man Killed	Kingdoms of this world become kingdoms of God Time of the dead/judged Rewards to the servants	Destroy those who Destroy the Earth

Earthquake (vertical, at 7th Trumpet)

Revelation 7 –Parenthetical

A great Multitude Comes out of Great Tribulation	Great Multitude Before the Throne. No More Tears

144,000 sealed
← before
1st trumpet

5th seal	**6th Seal**	**7th Seal**
Souls Slain for their Testimony	Day of the Lamb	Silence in Heaven

Great Earthquake / *sun/moon stars/darkened* (vertical, at 6th Seal)

Antichrist Rises/ Great Tribulation	**Church Rapture**	**Battle of Armageddon**	**Millennial Reign of Christ**
1260 days	30 days	45 days	

"blessed is he who comes to the 1335...

Day of the Lord begins...

Paul's Post Position

In nurturing the infant church, the apostle Paul ultimately ended up writing close to half the books found within the New Testament. Two were directed toward the church at Thessalonica. Due to unrelenting persecutions and tribulations, there were certain Thessalonians who had become troubled over rumors that they had somehow missed Christ's gathering of the church and as a consequence, unknowingly thrust into the time of God's wrath. When Paul learned of it, he quickly sent them a second letter specifically to counter this notion, and to reestablish the doctrine he had originally relayed to them in person. This follow-up letter, if interpreted correctly, provides one of the most conclusive proofs concerning Paul's positioning of the church *rapture* and the return of Jesus Christ.

Paul immediately begins his campaign against false doctrine by specifically addressing those Thessalonians who were troubled over the return of Christ.

II Thessalonians 1:7-9
*7**And to you who are troubled** rest with us, when the Lord Jesus shall be revealed from heaven with his mighty angels,*
8In flaming fire taking vengeance on them that know not God, and that obey not the gospel of our Lord Jesus Christ:
9Who shall be punished with everlasting destruction from the presence of the Lord, and from the glory of his power;

Most agree that what Paul is describing between verses 7 and 9 is the Second Coming of Christ after the great tribulation. It's the day of His wrath at the battle of Armageddon. What must be immediately considered is this: If Paul was truly a pre-tribulation *rapture* proponent, why does he not comfort the troubled Thessalonians with that hope instead? This would have been a perfect opportunity to speak about exemption from the great tribulation yet Paul forgoes any mention of it, choosing only to describe the post-tribulation return. Why such emphasis on the post-tribulation return? Reading on:

II Thessalonians 1:10-11
10When he shall come to be glorified in his saints, and to be admired in all them that believe (because our testimony among you was believed) in that day.
*11Wherefore also we pray always for you, that our **God would count you worthy of this calling**,*

In verse 12, Paul's prayer for the Thessalonians is that they are counted worthy of "this calling"—but to what calling is he referring? Within the confines of strict contextual interpretation, it is the calling of Christ being glorified in you in "that day." Which day is that? Again, adhering to the context in operation, it is the day that Christ returns in flaming fire to take vengeance on those who don't obey the gospel—*a strict post-tribulation event.* An obvious inconsistency in the pre-tribulation theory immediately manifests here by considering that if the church was truly *raptured* off the planet seven years, or even three and a half years prior to this particular day, then we would have *already been accounted worthy of this calling.* However, it's clear in chapter one that he's not talking about a secret *rapture* prior to this day. Paul tells us that we should pray to be accounted worthy on "that day"—Christ's post-tribulation return with vengeance. The reason Paul is placing so much emphasis on the post-tribulation return right from the beginning of his letter is because he believes that the church is to remain present on earth until that day comes!

Even more intriguing evidence begins to present itself with the realization that Paul is actually citing Scripture from another area of the New Testament.

Luke 21:36
*Watch ye therefore, and **pray always, that ye may be accounted worthy** to escape all these things that shall come to pass, and to stand before the Son of man.*

This verse can be found on the frontlines of the pre-tribulation *rapture* theory battlefield, and has become a weapon of choice. I can't tell you how many times it's been lobbed at me! Certainly, when viewing this verse through their eyes, the word *escape* is a fitting choice to propagate an early *rapture* of the church. However, the Greek counterpart to the word "escape" is "ekpheugó" and is defined as "to flee away." This is in stark contrast to the Greek words used for "caught up," "changed," "gather," or "taken" which the Bible actually utilizes as a reference to the true *rapture* of the church. It is in the writer's opinion that "fleeing away" would be a poor way to describe a victorious church rising to meet a world-conquering Savior no matter what language you speak!

In truth, the escape to which Christ was referring was a "fleeing away"—*on earth*—from a long list of events that He provided His disciples in response to their question of "what will be the sign of your coming?" Wars, famine, diseases, and earthquakes are just some of the frightening episodes He reveals to be precursors to His Second Advent. Then, in Luke 21:27, Jesus describes how He will return after these particular events unfold.

Luke 21:27
And then shall they see the Son of man coming in a cloud with power and great glory.

It should be noted that Luke 21 is a mirror passage to Matthew 24, and that Christ is speaking of His post-tribulation return here, after which we come across the last statement of Jesus in Luke 21:36 that pre-tribulation advocates rush to quote, but that Paul cites in his second letter to the Thessalonians in a completely different context setting.

Jesus provides two parts to Luke 21: the events that will take place prior to His arrival, and then a description of the arrival itself. Likewise, Luke 21:36 is to be understood in the same manner. It's the very last statement Jesus makes and is simply a single verse conclusion to the entire preceding passage of Luke 21. The first part of the verse deals with the events that will signify His soon return: "pray always, that you may be accounted worthy to escape" (or flee away from) wars, diseases, famine, etc.... Then Jesus adds: "AND to stand before the Son of Man." "And" is a keyword because it separates the verse into two sections just as He did previously in His description. If I was to say to you: Brother or sister, pray that I make it through this trial I'm currently experiencing in my life, and to have peace of mind. Am I asking for one prayer request or two? The answer is, of course, two. Pray that I make it through this trial, AND also pray that I have peace of mind. Likewise, Christ formulates His conclusion in the same manner:

> *"pray always, that you may be accounted worthy to escape* (flee away from*) all these things that shall come to pass, AND* (pray that you may be accounted worthy) *to stand before the Son of man."*

This conclusion directly conflicts with the pre-tribulation view because if Jesus was actually inferring a *rapture* of the church by using the word "escape," we would have already been accounted worthy to stand before the Son of man!

Additionally, since Jesus predefines a post-tribulation return by the Son of man in Luke 21:27 and the latter half of Luke 21:36 is merely a conclusion to that event, then to "stand before the Son of man" is the true reference to the *rapture* of the church. A person can only stand if he has a body. This initially indicates that the resurrection of the dead is to take place at His post-tribulation coming where the souls of heaven will be reunited with their bodies in glorified form. Since the Bible is explicit in teaching that the *rapture* can only take place after the resurrection of the dead, then the living believers will experience a similar translation, receiving a glorified body in lieu of their present earthly one.

Fortunately, this is fully validated in Revelation 7:9 where John, in his revelation, foresees a great multitude *standing before the throne on the post-tribulation day of the Lamb*. The throne is none other than the glorious throne of Jesus Christ which will be raised up in Jerusalem and is where the Son of man will separate the nations in the sheep/goat judgment. Then, He will rule the world with a rod of iron for 1000 years. The great multitude consists of those who will partake in the resurrection and *rapture* event. They will stand before Him in great reverence for their Savior with palms in their hands and victorious shouts of praise in their mouths—an evident recapture of Christ's first entry into Jerusalem as King just a week before His crucifixion.

The fact that Paul quotes Luke 21:36 within the strict confines of Christ's post-tribulation return he had meticulously laid out in the first chapter of II Thessalonians is obviously overlooked, and exposes a huge piece of evidence that Christ's intent was the same in Luke 21:36, and in no way was either one making an inference to a pre-tribulation *rapture* of the church. On the contrary, Paul realized the quick strangle-hold false doctrine was beginning to put on the Thessalonian church. In response, he took extremely careful measure to establish the context of his entire second letter by explaining well known aspects of Christ's *post-tribulation return* in chapter one that, in truth, are to be *carried into chapter 2* if we are to interpret correctly. This simple yet important fact brings the first verse of chapter 2 into a whole new light when applying this foundational principle of scriptural interpretation.

II Thessalonians 2:1
Now we beseech you, brethren, by the coming of our
Lord Jesus Christ, and by our gathering together
unto him,

The one million dollar question is this: *Which coming and gathering is he referring to here?* Curiously, pre-tribulation advocates try to apply the secret *rapture* of the church to this verse, but did Paul secretly switch topics? If the Thessalonians were in total confusion about the timing of Christ's return for the church, would it actually have been logical for Paul to pull a fast switch at this juncture about a gentle secret *rapture* seven years prior to the Second Coming without first clearly describing it in vivid pre-tribulation detail? Truly, if his intent for verse 1 was that of a pre-tribulation event, then it would have been highly probable he would have had to send a third letter to clear that mess up as well because they would have been even more baffled! Remember, he had just finished explaining to the utterly confused Thessalonians certain aspects of Christ's Second Coming after the great tribulation in chapter one for one specific reason—to clean up any tiny bit of confusion about His return in relation to the church's salvation. Since there is absolutely no mention of a secret *rapture* anywhere, then the Bible must be allowed to define itself. This is accomplished correctly through the avenue of context. *Paul was merely carrying his message from chapter one into chapter two.* He assumed the Thessalonians would make this easy connection between the two chapters and recognize his intent (which they did because there isn't a third letter!).

-The Day of Christ-

Into verse 2, Paul writes:

That ye be not soon shaken in mind, or be troubled, neither by spirit, nor by word, nor by letter as from us, as that the **day of Christ** *is at hand.*

The Authorized King James Version, completed and published in 1611, was translated from the Textus Receptus series of the Greek New Testament texts, and in II Thessalonians 2:2 encounters the name "Χριστός," which is interpreted as "the anointed one" or "Messiah"—a direct and specific reference to Christ. The Authorized King James version honored this interpretation by adhering to the term "day of Christ" in its translation. This particular "day of Christ" term of II Thessalonians 2:2 is correctly interpreted by pretribulation advocates as a post-tribulation event, but is incorrectly separated from the *rapture* of the church because of the overlooked context of Christ's post-tribulation coming in chapter 2 verse 1—set by the previous chapter. This separation is absolutely necessary in order to uphold a pretribulation *rapture* of the church because the chapter goes on to list certain events that must unfold before the day of Christ can come. If the *rapture* was to occur on this day, it would destroy the imminent return of Jesus and mandate the rise of the Antichrist as a prequel to the *rapture*. Obviously this would present a major discrepancy!

However, Scofield, a forefather to the pre-tribulation theory and famous for his Scofield Study Bible, saw another predicament quickly rising to the surface here. He knew that any other encounter with the term "day of Christ" within the New Testament was quickly associated by pre-tribulation theorists with the pre-tribulation *rapture* of the

116

church. He realized that if they were caught in a pick-and-choose approach, it could be detrimental to the theory by displaying its inconsistencies. In an attempt to recover, he decides to revert to the older and more obscure Alexandrian text type of the Greek manuscript (where some of the more modern translations are derived) which translates this same verse to the "day of the Lord" rather than "day of Christ." He then makes a claim in his reference notes that the Authorized King James version "has the day of Christ incorrectly for the day of the Lord" (The Scofield Reference Bible, copyright 1917, page 1212). Since pre-tribulation theorists view the day of the Lord as a day of vengeful judgment that is wholly disconnected from the day of Christ, then this term change would seemingly alleviate the pressure that II Thessalonians 2:2 was beginning to place on them, and ultimately disconnect their pre-tribulation *rapture* from any post-tribulation implications.

However, while Scofield was busy splitting hairs over II Thessalonians 2:2, I Corinthians 5:5 was laying in silent ambush.

I Corinthians 5:5
*To deliver such an one unto Satan for the destruction of the flesh, that the spirit may be saved in the **day of the Lord Jesus**.*

Unfortunately, what Scofield had quickly forgotten is that he had made a small note in his subject reference margin concerning the above verse in regards to the term "day of the Lord Jesus" that "some ancient authorities omit Jesus" (page 1216). It was clear from his previous reference notes of page 1212 that he was *now against* this particular omission because he claimed II Thessalonians 2:2 to be the *only* incorrect translation and actually adds this verse of I

Corinthians 5:5 in the list of correct "day of Christ" translations. Yet, the "ancient authorities" he was so adamantly against in I Corinthians 5:5 because of their omission of Jesus from the day of the Lord, are the same "ancient authorities" he attempts in leveraging to his advantage in II Thessalonians 2:2 because of the very same reason! By admitting that the day of Jesus Christ *should* be attributed to the day of the Lord in I Corinthians, he directly contradicts himself concerning II Thessalonians! As you can see, Scofield's meddling with the "day of Christ" term of II Thessalonians 2:2 was merely a desperate attempt to maintain a viewpoint that had been backed into a corner. This interpretation error begins to shed light on the pre-tribulation *rapture* theory as a whole, leaving it a major suspect of fraud. It becomes more that just a viable point that if self-imposing contradictions, such as the one exposed here, are being used as a foundation to build this doctrine, then it's more than likely that the doctrine itself is contradictory to Scripture as well.

Ironically, Scofield was actually closer to the truth than he realized. The day of Christ term found in II Thessalonians 2:2 is, in fact, speaking about the day of the Lord. However, what he, and all other pre-tribulation *rapture* believers continually fail to recognize, is that *any* encounter with the term "day of Christ" in the New Testament is speaking about the post-tribulation day of the Lord event, whether it be in II Thessalonians 2:2 or elsewhere. Likewise, any encounter with term "day of the Lord," whether found in the Old or New Testament, is speaking about the day of Christ, making Scofield's overly critiqued presentation of translation discrepancies irrelevant from the very start. The proof rests in a quick study of Jehovah's day.

Isaiah 13:9,10
*⁹Behold, the **day of the LORD** cometh, cruel both with wrath and fierce anger, to lay the land desolate: and he shall destroy the sinners thereof out of it.*
*¹⁰For the **stars of heaven** and the constellations thereof shall **not give their light**: **the sun shall be darkened** in his going forth, and the **moon shall not cause her light to shine**.*

Jesus sets a timeline for the day of the Lord by describing the exact same astronomical signs in Matthew 24:

Matthew 24:29
***Immediately after the tribulation** of those days shall the **sun be darkened**, and the **moon shall not give her light**, and the **stars shall fall from heaven**, and the powers of the heavens shall be shaken*

As you can see, the Old Testament day of the Lord will be marked by a supernatural darkening of the heavens immediately after the great tribulation. If we turn to Revelation chapter six and dissect the sixth seal, a very important factor begins to emerge.

Revelation 6:12-13
*¹²And I beheld when he had opened the sixth seal, and, lo, there was a great earthquake; and the **sun became black** as sackcloth of hair, and the **moon became as blood**;*
*¹³And the **stars of heaven fell** unto the earth,...*

Again, we encounter the exact same celestial events that Jesus explained would only occur immediately after the great tribulation, and that the Old Testament reveals as specific markers for the day of the Lord. What is the second piece of information that the sixth seal reveals?

Revelation 6:16-17
*16And said to the mountains and rocks, Fall on us, and hide us from the face of him that sitteth on the throne, and from the **wrath of the Lamb**:*
*17For the **great day of his wrath is come**; and who shall be able to stand?*

The <u>day of Christ</u> has come! The Lamb is a specific reference to Christ! First, this proves without any doubt that the Old Testament day of the Lord <u>is</u> the New Testament day of Christ where Jehovah's day will manifest as Christ's return in fiery vengeance to lay the land desolate. Second, the day of Christ is a *strict post-tribulation event* (just as Paul had stated in II Thess. 2:3). Jesus verifies this fact in Luke 17:30 by claiming the post-tribulation day of the Lord to be "the day when the Son of man is revealed." Of course, the "Son of man" is a reference to Christ thus uniting the Old Testament day of the Lord with the day of Christ once more. In relation, whether using translations derived from the old Alexandrian text type which uses the term "day of the Lord" in the New Testament, or whether using translations from the Textus Receptus which defines the Lord as Christ matters not because it's all classified under one unified post-tribulation event.

This important information brings one other immensely critical factor to the surface. Since Scripture clearly defines the term "day of Christ" as a strict post-tribulation event in every area, with the most notable found in Matthew 24:29-

31, Mark 13:24-27, Luke 17:24, Luke 21:25-27, II Thessalonians 1:7-9, II Thessalonians 2:2, Revelation 6:12-17, and Revelation 19:11-16, and that *nowhere* in Scripture can a literal description of a pre-tribulation day of Christ be found (that fact alone should be enough to destroy the idea of a pre-tribulation return), then *any* encounter with this term must be respected as a post-tribulation event in every instance—a fundamental rule of scriptural interpretation. With that in mind, consider the following passage:

> *Philippians 2:14-16*
> *14Do all things without murmurings and disputings:*
> *15That ye may be blameless and harmless, the sons of God, without rebuke, in the midst of a crooked and perverse nation, among whom ye shine as lights in the world;*
> *16Holding forth the word of life; that I may rejoice in the **day of Christ**, that I have not run in vain, neither labored in vain.*

Infiltrating Paul's mindset concerning how he viewed the next return of Christ is simple to determine because it was evident from his teachings. Here, Paul admonished the Philippians to abstain from frivolous arguing and to hold up the Word in their daily lives as the guide to better living so that he may rejoice for them in the *day of Christ*. Again, the Bible pre-defines this day as a strict post-tribulation event. As an expert in scriptural interpretation, Paul would have been required to adhere to the critical Scripture-defines-Scripture rule, respect the day of Christ in this manner, and carry this view into *all* his letters. He clearly does this, for example, in the first part of his second letter to the Thessalonians where he vividly described the day of Christ in fiery, vengeance-filled detail—an obvious post-tribulation reference to any reader. Therefore, the question that can be posed is this: Why does Paul have to wait until the post-tribulation day of Christ to rejoice as stated in Philippians? Wouldn't a pre-tribulation *rapture* of the church give him the validation he needs already? Why would Paul have to wait *in heaven* for seven years for the post-tribulation day of Christ to manifest before he could actually rejoice over the church if the collective church had already experienced a pre-tribulation *rapture* and was standing right next to him? The answer is—he wouldn't! It's because Paul knows his day of validation and confirmation will not come until the post-tribulation day of Christ.

Philippians 1:6 addresses Christ's day once again:

Philippians 1:6
*Being confident of this very thing, that he which hath begun a good work in you will perform it until the **day of Jesus Christ**:*

Paul's eschatological view comes into sharp focus once more by associating Christ's next return with the post-tribulation day of Christ. He believes that the church will remain on earth until that day comes, evident by how he addresses the Philippians in this verse.

-*Why were they shaken?*-

If the "day of Christ" term is seated in II Thessalonians 2:2 correctly, and that day is to include the church's gathering and glorification, then why did Paul plead with the Thessalonians not to be "shaken in mind" that this particular day might be "at hand?" Wouldn't the idea of an imminent *rapture* instill comfort instead? Shouldn't they have been waiting in joyous anticipation? Why were they still troubled?

In truth, the reason they were still experiencing such anxiety was because the Thessalonians understood the concept of salvation and wrath occurring on the same day that Jesus returns. This understanding, without doubt, would have originated with Paul's first letter to them. There, he explained in I Thessalonians chapter 5, that the day of the Lord will overtake the world like a thief and experience the unrelenting wrath of God, but as for the church, she is not appointed to this wrath because of the salvation that will come in the form of the *rapture* on that *same day*. This same-day conclusion would have easily been made by the Thessalonians because Paul had initially connected the *rapture*—described in I Thessalonians 4:16-17—to the post-tribulation day of the Lord in I Thessalonians 5:2. This reveals that the salvation of the church and God's wrath against the wicked are both to occur on that day (and in that order), of which, he merely reiterates in I Thessalonians 5:9-10. While pre-tribulation believers consider the post-tribulation day of the Lord/Christ of II Thessalonians 2:2 to be a strict wrath-filled event, in truth, *both salvation and wrath are to occur on that day together.*

Paul revisits this fact here in his second letter to the Thessalonians by first describing the wrath of Christ on the post-tribulation day of Christ in chapter one between verses 7 and 9, but also includes the church's glorification which is to come about on that *same day*—described in verse 10.

Christ absolutely verified this concept in Matthew 24 when utilizing the cross reference of Noah to explain His Second Coming. While the wicked were subjected to the wrath of God in the great flood, Noah *simultaneously* experienced salvation within the confines of the ark and was supernaturally shut in by God Himself. Likewise, when Christ returns on the day of the Lord after the great tribulation, the elect, like Noah, will be gathered again, experiencing another supernatural "shut-in," while the wicked *on that same day* are to be trod down in His great wrath.

Although John in Revelation initially describes the post-tribulation sixth seal from the perspective of the day of the Lord/Lamb's wrath, he too, soon after, describes a large resurrection which will occur at that same time. This exposes the plain fact of a salvation/wrath event on the day of the Lord once more.

This theme was not limited to the New Testament because Joel adhered to the same concept as well:

Joel 3:15-16
15The sun and the moon shall be darkened, and the stars shall withdraw their shining.
16The LORD also shall roar out of Zion, and utter his voice from Jerusalem; and the heavens and the earth shall shake: **but the LORD will be the hope of his people, and the strength of the children of Israel.**

Joel, towards the end of his prophecy, again described the day of the Lord from a celestial standpoint, stating that the heavens and the earth will shake at that time. This shaking is to be a fierce shaking under the wrath of God Almighty (Isaiah 13:13), but notice as this frightening episode unfolds, Joel thankfully adds that the Lord will be the "hope of his people, and the strength of the children of Israel" at that same time. Again, wrath and salvation are placed together under one unified event.

Even though the Thessalonians understood this concept, they had still become "shaken in mind" because they thought they had missed the first part of Christ's day entailing the *rapture* of the church, and unwillingly cast into the second portion containing wrath that is to be poured out immediately after. Therefore, the day of Christ had become a dreaded event. Even though Paul had repeatedly told them in his first letter, and also once in II Thessalonians chapter one (vs. 7-11) that they are not to fear being subjected to God's wrath simply because of the *rapture* that the church is to experience on that day, Paul, in his infinite patience, attacks the misconception that they had somehow missed it and essentially tells them in II Thessalonians 2:1-2: *Regarding the coming of Christ and the rapture of the church, don't be troubled that you've missed it, because that day of Christ isn't here yet.*

-*The Identity of the Restrainer*-

Up to this point, Paul had taken special care in chapter 1 by describing the post-tribulation day of Christ between verses 7-9 and then connecting the gathering of the church to that same day in verse 10. This was followed by Paul's prayer that they be "accounted worthy of this calling" in verse 11, all of which was used as a spring board for chapter 2. There, he begins setting an important prophetic timeline for the day of Christ as a guideline to help the Thessalonians (and us) understand when this epic day would occur.

> *II Thessalonians 2:3-4*
> *3Let no man deceive you by any means: for that day (day of Christ) shall not come, except there come a falling away first, and that man of sin be revealed, the son of perdition;*
> *4Who opposeth and exalteth himself above all that is called God, or that is worshipped; so that he as God sitteth in the temple of God, shewing himself that he is God.*

In the first four verses of chapter 2, Paul writes about three events, and gives the specific order in which they are to unfold:

1> The Falling Away (apostasy)
2> The Antichrist Revealed
3> The Day of Christ and our Gathering unto Him (*rapture*)

Of course, it now becomes clearly evident why the term "day of Christ" of verse 3 is attacked with such vigor by pre-tribulation advocates because, if interpreted correctly, it is overwhelmingly devastating to the theory since it places the *rapture* of the church after the rise of the Antichrist—an event that is to take place throughout the great tribulation. Continuing into verse 6, Paul then writes:

*⁶And now ye know what **withholdeth** that he might be revealed in his time.*

Upon establishing the three major end time events, Paul immediately makes the statement (paraphrased): "and now you know what is restraining the appearance of the Antichrist" (this is the context in operation at this point). But why does Paul make that assumption? While many assume the Thessalonians may have already been aware of this information because Paul addressed it upon a previous physical visitation to the church, it would have actually been illogical for Paul to make such a bold statement without first citing the Antichrist's true restraining force within his letter when considering that the Thessalonians were in complete confusion and the whole point of this letter was to provide clarity. In truth, the reason Paul made such a statement with absolute confidence is because he had *just* addressed it only a few verses earlier. The Thessalonians knew of the true restraining force at this point in the letter because he had *just finished explaining it to them in verse 3*: Before the man of sin can be revealed, *a falling away must come first.*

In reality, verse 6 was not an assumption statement thrown without caution into the wind in hopes that the Thessalonians would catch it with full understanding. Instead, it was merely a short recap on an already-established truth within his letter. It would be like me saying to you: *"John Doe has just announced his candidacy for a run at the White House; however, he must first campaign aggressively and convince the public of his qualifications. And now you know what is withholding John Doe from becoming the next U.S. President."* The reason you now know is because it was just explained to you: Before John Doe can become president, *he must first campaign aggressively.* Likewise, Paul establishes the identity of the restrainer in verse 3 and then almost immediately reminds the Thessalonians in verse 6: "So now you know what restrains the Antichrist [because I just finished explaining it to you. Before the man of sin can be revealed, a falling away must come first."] Many fail to recognize that _this_ is where the restrainer's true identity is actually established and not further along in the chapter.

Additional proof rests in the fact that the restrainer in verse 6 is specifically addressed as a "what" and not a "who." *This completely disqualifies the restrainer from being a particular personality but rather an event.* That event is the falling away! More importantly, verse 6 now becomes the context-setter in relation to the identity of the restrainer that is to be carried throughout the rest of the chapter if we are to interpret correctly. Paul begins to elaborate on this fact in the very next verse:

7For the mystery of iniquity doth already work:

After stating "and now you know what is withholding the Antichrist," Paul immediately affirms: "For the mystery of iniquity already works." This provides clear and much-needed confirmation that the true restraining force is actually the presently working falling away. Then he adds:

...only he who now letteth will let, until he be taken out of the way.

This small sentence ending has become one of the most widely debated in mainstream circles with multiple claims coming forward about who the "he" is in this verse. However, to get a true definition, the context of the passage must be adhered to without wavering. Remember, Paul had just listed three major events at the beginning of the chapter, giving them a specific order. He started with the falling away apostasy—which must come first, followed by the Satanic rise of the Antichrist, and then the highly anticipated day of Christ. Verse 7 is simply the beginning of a series of subsequent verses that were designed to describe these three events in their respective order and in further detail, starting with an initial description of the falling away (withholder of verse 6).

1> **The Falling Away**
7For the mystery of iniquity doth already work: only he who now letteth will let, until he be taken out of the way.

The confusion over verse 7 stems from the fact that the "he" is a personal pronoun—a seeming reference to a particular individual. The temptation is to insert whoever "fits your bill" the best here (i.e. the Holy Spirit/Church), but again, we must rely on the passage to do that for us. Otherwise, it has just become speculation. Speculative interpretation produces speculative doctrine.

The Greek word for "letteth" is katecho (kat-ekh'-o). Among others, it is defined as *to hinder*, or *to withhold*. Since Paul already pre-defined <u>what</u> the withholder was in verse 3 (it was not a particular individual, but instead, the falling away apostasy), then we are required to adhere to that established truth throughout the entire chapter *and verse 7 is no exception*. Therefore, what Paul was simply stating here is that the "he" is one—*of many*— who are part of the true restraining force—the current falling away!

When Paul wrote about the "he," he was simply taking an overall event, breaking it down, and describing it on an individual level. It would be like me saying to you: *"Congress is considering legislation that would require Americans to pay even more taxes* (overall description of the event). *Only <u>he</u> who supports this bill will lose more of his money"* (individual description of the overall event). Yes, it's individualized, and yes, it utilizes a personal pronoun, but clearly the "he" is not there to portray a particular personality. *It's there to help describe a certain event.* That event is the transfer of more money to the government by American citizens. In relation to II Thessalonians chapter two, that event is the falling away apostasy, and the "he" is simply an individualized description of what will ultimately fulfill that event. This rests in absolute harmony with the already-established restrainer of verse 3 and conforms to the context of the entire passage.

So how does "he" hinder the Antichrist's appearance? Look at the verse it's situated in...by allowing the mystery of iniquity to work *in himself,* thus fulfilling his part in the falling away until its completion. How is "he" finally removed? Since the subject concerns a falling away from the truth of the gospel, then "he" is finally removed once "he" has been completely severed from the truth! By rejecting God's Word, "he" will have become conditioned by sin to accept a worldly way of thinking, a counterfeit gospel, and a false sense of security; "he" will have become absolutely ripe for a major global delusion.

Only once this Satanic apostasy has completely removed all those appointed to be removed from the truth of the gospel, and those with the testimony of Jesus Christ have become the minority can the Antichrist truly rise to power because at that point, there will be enough people who have fallen away to actually accept this man of sin as their leader and their false messiah.

Initially, it might seem irrational that those who allow the mystery of iniquity to work in themselves could be restraining the Wicked One, but by simply thinking objectively: Could the Antichrist truly rise to power if the majority of the world were genuine Bible believers? Of course, the answer is no. He would be recognized immediately as his true nature would be exposed by us all. In that way, Satan must first deceive the masses into something other than the truth in order to grasp the power he needs.

Right now, Satan is campaigning aggressively for the arrival of the Antichrist, but he must wait until the right time to bring his leader forward, otherwise, he will be immediately rejected. Thus, the restrainer (the hinderer and withholder), is the progressive apostasy that must come into fullness first. This completion will then allow Satan to safely bring his "man of sin" onto the world scene as the false messiah in mockery of the true Christ because the majority will be, at that point, _removed from the truth_.

I am fully aware that many of you, for so long, have been taught otherwise, so this concept might be hard to comprehend at first. Fortunately, the book of Daniel solidifies the identity of the restrainer, making it absolutely undeniable what Paul is trying to express to the Thessalonian church.

Daniel 8:23
*And in the latter time of their kingdom, when the **transgressors are come to the full**, a king of fierce countenance, and understanding dark sentences, shall stand up.*

The "king of fierce countenance" is a reference to the end time Antichrist who, according to Daniel, is being *withheld* until the falling away has "come to the full." Consider it in this way: Could the Antichrist stand up if the transgressors have not come to the full? If we claim Scripture as the final authority, then the answer has to be no. *Therefore, he is restrained scripturally until the falling away has been fulfilled.* This is the true restraining force withholding the Antichrist from being revealed! Once sin abounds in the allotted amount of humanity, then—and only then— can the Antichrist rise. Does that sound like the world today? If we look around us, it is clear that this falling away from the truth, en mass, is extremely close to completion, and that we will soon witness the rise of this Satanic super power. This present progressive apostasy is the only event truly withholding the Antichrist from bringing himself into full view <u>until its completion,</u> and *then* he will finally be allowed to stand up according to Scripture.

The next verse in II Thessalonians 2 simply continues with its respective descriptions Paul initially laid out in verse 3.

2> Antichrist Revealed
8And then shall that Wicked be revealed,...

Finally, a description of the third event:

3> Second Coming of Christ
⁸...whom the Lord shall consume with the spirit of his mouth, and shall destroy with the brightness of his coming:

If I haven't convinced you that the currently working falling away apostasy restrains the appearance of the Antichrist until its completion, then read on because Paul, *for a third time*, immediately reiterates that the Antichrist will only come once the falling away has claimed all of its victims. He merely starts with the second event first and describes it as coming after the first, thus placing it in its correct order.

2>Antichrist Revealed
*⁹Even him (Antichrist), whose coming is **after** the working of Satan with all power and signs and lying wonders,*

1>The Falling Away
¹⁰And with all deceivableness of unrighteousness in them that perish; because they received not the love of the truth, that they might be saved. 11 And for this cause God shall send them strong delusion, that they should believe a lie: 12 That they all might be damned who believed not the truth, but had pleasure in unrighteousness.

Verse 10 undeniably points out the true restraining force once more and again adheres to the context first established in verses 3 and 6, allowing it to rest in perfect harmony with verse 7, and with the prophecy found in the book of Daniel. Notice that there is absolutely no mention of the Holy Spirit being taken out here. Instead, a sober reminder is given that the cost of falling away from the good news of the gospel is great and once removed from the truth, the only thing remaining is strong delusion which will be sent from God Himself as an initial sentencing to their ultimate demise. It is *this* event that Paul deems as the Antichrist's true withholder, stating in verse 3 that it "must come first," and that Daniel wrote must come to <u>fullness</u> before the "king of fierce countenance" can stand up.

Paul then nicely sums up the chapter by recounting the return of Christ and our gathering to Him for a third time.

3>Second Coming of Christ and our Gathering unto Him (*rapture*).

*13But we are bound to give thanks alway to God for you, brethren beloved of the Lord, because God hath from the beginning chosen you to salvation through sanctification of the Spirit and belief of the truth: 14Whereunto he called you by our gospel, **to the obtaining of the glory of our Lord Jesus Christ**.*

A major key to understanding the timing of the church *rapture* in II Thessalonians chapter 2 rests in the pivotal role that verse 14 plays in relation to verse 3. Again, in verse 3, Paul had established the theme of his entire passage (context) that is merely echoed throughout the rest of the chapter. Remember, three events were listed there and given a specific order of occurrence: The falling away, the rise of the Antichrist, and lastly, the day of Christ. Considering that verses 7 and 8 merely echo that sentiment, followed by a *third* reiteration of verse 3 found between verses 9 and 14, then a major error in the pre-tribulation theory manifests once more and it's found in verse 14. When studying the overlay of these verses, the first thing to be found is that verse 14 is indisputably referencing the post-tribulation day of Christ first mentioned in verse 3. This is further verified by the statement: "the glory of our Lord Jesus Christ." This is a glory that Paul specifically attributed to Christ's post-tribulation arrival—discussed in the first chapter (II Thess. 1:9), and then verified in II Thessalonians 2:8 (among many other areas of Scripture). Notice that as Paul is describing this particular day in verse 14 from a third perspective, *he also includes the church's glorification at that same time* (just as he had in chapter 1 verse 10). This letter was written to the church in Thessalonica and to the church of Christ in general. Why does he mention the church's glorification here? *It's because Paul equated the church's gathering and glorification with the post-tribulation day of Christ.*

This overlooked piece of crucial evidence renders frivolous arguments about the church being taken out prior to the Second Coming of Christ absolutely invalid and completely disqualifies the present day church as a possible candidate for the restrainer. Instead, staying true to the layout of his chapter, Paul leaves the description of the church's glorification for last because he wanted to avoid any possible confusion by making sure that everything was explained in its exact order of occurrence.

Without question, Paul was a post-tribulation preacher and took every measure to convince the Thessalonians they hadn't missed the gathering because two events must unfold prior to Christ's return in vengeance and the church's salvation into glory.

The 3 Themes	II Thessalonians 2:3	II Thessalonians 2:7-8	II Thessalonians 2:9-10,14
The Falling Away	³ Let no man deceive you by any means: for that day shall not come, except there come a falling away first,	⁷ For the mystery of iniquity doth already work: only he who now letteth will let, until he be taken out of the way.	⁹ Even him whose coming is after the working of Satan... ¹⁰ And with all deceivableness of unrighteousness in them that perish; because they received not the love of the truth, that they might be saved.
Antichrist Revealed	and that man of sin be revealed, the son of perdition;	⁸ And then shall that Wicked be revealed, *(Antichrist comes after the falling away apostasy)*	
The Day of Christ (post)	(The day of Christ won't come until the above two have come to pass)	whom the Lord shall consume with the spirit of his mouth, and shall destroy with the brightness of his coming:	¹⁴ Whereunto he called __YOU__ by our gospel, to the **obtaining of the glory of our Lord Jesus Christ.**

Paul, in his third reiteration of verse 3, equates the church's glorification with the post-trib day of Christ.

The Path to Wrath

One of the first arguments raised by pre-tribulation believers when confronted with the notion that the church will see the great tribulation is: *How can the church be included in this time period if we are not appointed to God's wrath?* This seems to be *the* foremost area of confusion when it comes to trying to understand the post-tribulation viewpoint and is one of the main reasons why it's quickly disregarded. I believe that this chapter is one of the most important ones for any pre-tribulation theorist because, if seriously considered, it provides conclusive evidence that the great tribulation is being grossly misidentified and that an unbiased scriptural definition of that short era is the key to shedding light on the truth.

So what truth do I speak of? Today, an *erroneous association* between the great tribulation period and the time of God's wrath has silently crept into the church which has created susceptibility to false doctrine, but the truth is, the Bible makes a definitive distinction between the two. I believe the root cause of this misunderstanding begins in I Thessalonians 5:9.

I Thessalonians 5:9
For God hath not appointed us to wrath, but to ob-
tain salvation by our Lord Jesus Christ,

Indeed, this verse is clear; believers will not be subjected to the wrath of God because of their faith in Jesus
Christ. But what is Paul actually talking about here? Is this
an inference to a one-way ticket out of the great tribulation? Is this implying a pre-tribulation *rapture* of the
church? As you may know by now, it is interpretation within the confines of context that allows the real truth to unfold, and here, when backing up to verse 2 within the
chapter, the true context is revealed for the remainder of
the passage.

I Thessalonians 5:2
*For yourselves know perfectly that the **day of the
Lord** so cometh as a thief in the night.*

What so many fail to recognize (or ignore) is that Paul
begins the passage by describing the day of the Lord which
immediately sets the context for the rest of the chapter.
Further study of subsequent verses under this unavoidable
and necessary rule produces a stunning conclusion.

I Thessalonians 5:4-9
*⁴But ye, brethren, are not in darkness, that that day
(The day of the Lord) should overtake you as a
thief.*
*⁵Ye are all the children of light, and the children of
the day: we are not of the night, nor of darkness*
*⁶Therefore let us not sleep, as do others; but let us
watch (for the day of the Lord) and be sober.*

7For they that sleep sleep in the night; and they that be drunken are drunken in the night.

8But let us, who are of the day, be sober, putting on the breastplate of faith and love; and for an helmet, the hope of salvation.

9For God hath not appointed us to wrath, but to obtain salvation by our Lord Jesus Christ.

When taking into consideration the actual context of the chapter, determining the message Paul is trying to convey comes into quick focus. Paul's point in I Thessalonians 5:9 is that believers are not subject to the wrath that will occur on the *day of the Lord*. While I have already provided many proofs that the day of the Lord is a strict post-tribulation event in other areas of this book, I will offer scriptural evidence once more.

Isaiah 13:9-10

*9Behold, the **day of the LORD** cometh, cruel both with **wrath and fierce anger**, to lay the land desolate: and he shall destroy the sinners thereof out of it.*

*10For the **stars of heaven and the constellations thereof shall not give their light: the sun shall be darkened** in his going forth, and the **moon shall not cause her light to shine**.*

Jesus establishes a strict post-tribulation timeline for the day of the Lord and the wrath of God that will occur on that particular day by describing the exact same celestial events in Matthew 24:29.

Immediately after the tribulation** of those days shall **the sun be darkened**, and the **moon shall

not give her light, *and the* **stars shall fall from heaven**, *and the powers of the heavens shall be shaken:*

By describing the exact celestial events that are clear indicators for the Old Testament day of the Lord, Jesus indirectly lays out indisputable evidence concerning the timing of that particular day. *It's time of arrival is strictly limited to some point after the great tribulation.* Therefore, Paul's message in I Thessalonians 5:9—a verse that is in strict context with that day—is that the church is to be spared from the wrath that will occur on the day of the Lord at the battle of Armageddon *immediately after the great tribulation, and has absolutely nothing to do with the great tribulation period whatsoever!* It is God Himself that has appointed us—not to wrath—but to salvation. But when does this salvation actually transpire? While the salvation being spoken of in verse 9 could be interpreted as a present salvation from sin (or a pre-tribulation *rapture*), again, the context of the passage actually dictates it to be a salvation from the wrath of God on the *post-tribulation day of the Lord.* How will this particular salvation unfold? Fortunately, it's addressed in the very next verse:

I Thessalonians 5:10
Who died for us, that, whether we **wake** *or* **sleep**, *we should live together with him.*

"Wake" and "sleep" is an undeniable reference to the resurrection and *rapture* of the church! It was Paul who had first established the *rapture* doctrine in I Thessalonians 4 by explaining it in a metaphorical "wake" and "sleep" format to help the church understand the mysteries of the *rapture* event better. When Christ returns, those who have slept (the dead in Christ) will be resurrected (verse 16), and those who are alive and remain (awake) will be *raptured* (verse 17). Without doubt, Paul plagiarized this descriptive style from the prophet Daniel who had used the terms "sleep" and "awake" in Daniel 12:2 when describing the resurrection of believers (of which, Daniel also sets in a post-tribulation timeframe).

By strictly adhering to the law of context, I Thessalonians chapter five, in its entirety, actually reveals that first and foremost, the church is not subject to the wrath of God that is to come about on the *post-tribulation day of the Lord*. Second, the method of salvation from this wrath is to be the manifestation of the resurrection and *rapture* which is to occur *on that day*. This is the very reason why Paul established a church mandate in verse 6 to be watching for the day of the Lord in the first place! It's because he identified this particular *rapture* salvation as *the* event that will spare the church from God's wrath on that very day.

-The First Revelation Verification-

To solidify this interpretation, multiple parallels can be found in the book Revelation. The first is found at the sixth seal. When the sixth seal is unveiled, John begins to witnesses celestial events that are to occur on the day of the Lord immediately after the great tribulation (Matt. 24:29, Isaiah 13:9-10).

Revelation 6:12-13
*12And I beheld when he had opened the sixth seal, and, lo, there was a great earthquake; and the **sun became black** as sackcloth of hair, and the **moon became as blood**;*

*13And the **stars of heaven fell** unto the earth, even as a fig tree casteth her untimely figs, when she is shaken of a mighty wind.*

This sets an identical subject content and timeframe to Paul's passage of I Thessalonians 5:2-10—where Paul mentioned the day of the Lord specifically. What else does the sixth seal reveal?

Revelation 6:15-17
15And the kings of the earth, and the great men, and the rich men, and the chief captains, and the mighty men, and every bondman, and every free man, hid themselves in the dens and in the rocks of the mountains;
*16And said to the mountains and rocks, Fall on us, and hide us from the face of him that sitteth on the throne, and from the **wrath of the Lamb**:*
*17For the **great day of his wrath is come**; and who shall be able to stand?*

First, the day of the Lamb's wrath *is* come. Again, the Greek manuscript associates with the wrath here strictly in the present tense. The reason for this present tense usage is to simply understand the function of a seal. A seal is exactly that—a seal. Its sole function is to *hide* the contents it contains until unloosed. Only once the seal is unloosed, can the contents of the seal finally be revealed. While this is basic reasoning, it must not be discarded when it comes to the seven seals of Revelation. The apostle John, at the beginning of his vision, wept over the fact that no one was worthy to open the seals. He wept because he desperately wanted to see what was contained within. It appears they were functioning as they should! The truth is, God's wrath on the day of the Lord is *sealed* <u>until</u> the sixth seal and cannot be unleashed until its unloosing. To make the claim that God's wrath can begin from the first seal onward is to also claim that the sixth seal didn't actually perform its duty of sealing God's wrath like it was suppose to—rendering it broken before Christ ever comes to unloose it. Since it's clear that the seven seals will only be unveiled in their chronological order, then it also becomes clear that God's day-of-the-Lord wrath can only be exposed at the sixth seal—a time that is clearly set by Matthew 24:29 in a strict post-tribulation timeframe. Like Paul's passage, God's wrath is again strictly associated with the day of the Lord at the sixth seal and is not unleashed until after the great tribulation.

Quickly, this reminds me of a time when I was listening to a pre-tribulation teacher on the radio who was presenting a case for the exclusion of the church from the great tribulation (because he said we are not appointed to God's wrath). He then carelessly quoted from this post-tribulation sixth seal as evidence of God's display of wrath *during* the great tribulation! Does he not realize that the seal he was using contains events that can only take place after the great tribulation? How can you make a case that the great tribulation is the time of God's wrath when you are extracting your main evidence from a post-tribulation seal? The answer is *you can't*—unless, of course, you have either missed, or have turned a blind eye to the obvious parallel between Revelation 6:12 and Matthew 24:29, and re-label it a period that occurs within the great tribulation to fit your own criteria!

Continuing on with the original point, the I Thessalonians 5/sixth seal parallel continues further:

Revelation 7:9,14
*⁹After this I beheld, and, lo, **a great multitude**, which no man could number, of all nations, and kindreds, and people, and tongues, stood before the throne, and before the Lamb, clothed with white robes, and palms in their hands;*
*¹⁴...these are they which came **out of great tribulation**, and have washed their robes, and made them white in the blood of the Lamb.*

John then goes on to describe an innumerable multitude of every nationality being swept up before the throne of God. This is the true church of Christ being resurrected and *raptured,* and spared from the wrath of God that is to occur on the day of the Lord—*just as Paul described it to be in I Thessalonians chapter 5.* When comparing the two passages, they are found to be identical because both describe the day of the Lord, the wrath of God, and a large gathering being saved on that day.

On another side note, this consistency brings to mind another vital interpretation tool often overlooked when determining whether a particular doctrine is trustworthy. That tool is comparing Scripture with Scripture. If a doctrine is found to be sitting in solitude scripturally, then it should be treated as highly suspect. However, if it can be literally verified in other areas, then all related passages must be interpreted together as a whole to identify the true message being conveyed. This tool works marvelously for I Thessalonians 4:16-5:10 because even though a pre-tribulation doctrine has been established there, the passage's evident interrelation with the post-tribulation sixth seal reveals the true timing of the *rapture* and its critical role on the day of the Lord.

-*The Second Revelation Verification*-

Since the sixth seal and seventh trumpet overlap each other and describe the same events only from different perspectives, it can be safely assumed that there's a reference at the last trumpet about the wrath of God finally manifesting just as there is at the sixth seal.

> *Revelation 11:18 (The Last Trump)*
> *And the nations were angry, and thy **wrath is come**, and **the time of the dead**, that they should be judged, and that thou shouldest give **reward unto thy servants** the prophets, **and to the saints**, and them that fear thy name, small and great; and shouldest **destroy them which destroy the earth**.*

Again, the same message is conveyed once more: God's wrath is come (the day of the Lord/day of Christ), the time of the dead has arrived (resurrection), rewards to the servants are issued out (*rapture*), and destruction is unleashed upon the wicked (Armageddon).

It must be noted at this juncture that, like the seals preceding the first mention of wrath at the sixth seal, there is absolutely no mention of Godly judgments or wrath in the six previous trumpet blasts either. Most err in thinking that all seven trumpets are a manifestation of God's wrath. I urge you to look it up for yourself because if you do, you won't find any literal mention of Godly judgments or wrath tied to the trumpets until the very last trumpet sound; and of course, that trumpet is a post-tribulation trumpet anyway. *Scripturally, the first six trumpets cannot be considered judgments or wrath from God.*

I use a Scofield Reference Bible and, unfortunately, Scofield labeled all the trumpets as "The Trumpet Judgments." It's absolutely incorrect and is also extremely misleading since the great tribulation begins at the fifth trumpet. This immediately paints a false picture that God is unleashing judgments/wrath throughout the course of the great tribulation period when, in fact, His wrath can only be manifested at the seventh and final trumpet blast. Once you begin to realize this information, it only further confirms the Greek's present tense interpretation of God's wrath at the seventh trumpet post-tribulation blast (and the sixth seal counterpart), and verifies that God's wrath begins after the great tribulation and at no other time.

-The Third Revelation Verification-

However, the withholding of God's judgment throughout the first six trumpets can be thoroughly verified in Revelation 14:7. There, it's finally revealed that the "hour of [God's] judgment is come." As discussed in a previous chapter, Revelation chapters 12 through 14 provide an accurate list of end time events in chronological order just like the seals and trumpets—only from a third perspective. It is displayed on the following page.

As shown in the above table, chapter 13 begins with the Beast's rise to power at the beginning of the great tribulation (in the middle of Daniel's seventieth week), and ends with the battle of Armageddon on the day of the Lord at the end of chapter 14.

Although this statement of God's judgment is found on a new timeline—separate from the trumpets' timeline, it is a statement that is still being clearly made well after the rise of the Antichrist and the False Prophet—two events that are catalysts for the great tribulation period. This makes God's judgment an obvious post-tribulation event. A simple translation of this information back to the seven trumpets' timeline <u>requires</u> the hour of God's judgment to be poured out *after* the fifth and sixth great tribulation trumpets because, there, the Beast rises out of the pit at the fifth trumpet and wars against the saints at the sixth. This clearly holds God's judgment to the last trumpet sound and provides solid proof of Scofield's label mismanagement of the first six trumpet blasts. It must also be emphasized that, like the seals and trumpets, the Revelation 12-14 timeline provides absolutely no evidence for a pouring out of Godly judgments or wrath throughout the course of the great tribulation.

-*The Messiah's Verification*-

In Matthew 24, Christ was also extremely specific in revealing a chronological timeline of end time events. He begins by first describing the great tribulation period.

> *Matthew 24:21*
> *For then shall be **great tribulation**, such as was not since the beginning of the world to this time, no, nor ever shall be.*

He then follows with a description concerning the *rapture* of the church:

> *Matthew 24:29, 31*
> *29**Immediately after the tribulation** of those days shall the sun be darkened, and the moon shall not give her light, and the stars shall fall from heaven, and the powers of the heavens shall be shaken:*
> *31And he shall send his angels with a great sound of a trumpet, and they shall **gather together his elect** from the four winds, from one end of heaven to the other.*

And lastly, a depiction of God's wrath:

Matthew 24:37-39
37But as the days of Noah were, so shall also the coming of the Son of man be.
38For as in the days that were before the flood they were eating and drinking, marrying and giving in marriage, until the day that Noe entered into the ark,
39And knew not until the flood came, and took them all away; so shall also the coming of the Son of man be.

It's widely accepted that the flood represents God's wrath here. However, many fail to see that Jesus strictly associates the flood of Noah's day (God's wrath) with His *Second Coming* which is to come about *after* the great tribulation. Although believers are to be correctly identified with Noah and likewise, the flood of Noah's day is to be associated with the wrath of God, this wrath has absolutely nothing to do with the great tribulation period because Jesus clearly applied the symbol of the great flood to His *post-tribulation descent only*.

Once again, another inconsistency in the pre-tribulation *rapture* theory quickly manifests. It's found in their repeated attempts to integrate the flood and what it represents with the great tribulation period. However, Jesus only connected the flood to His Second Coming after that time! Jesus *did not* claim: "and knew not until the flood came and took them all away, so shall also the coming of the great tribulation be" On the contrary, He stated: "so shall also the coming of the <u>Son of man</u> be!" Jesus had clearly declared, just moments earlier, that the Son of man will not descend from heaven until after the great tribulation—placing the analogy of the flood in a strict post-tribulation context.

The pre-tribulation theory erodes even further at this juncture because, on the one hand, great pains are taken in trying to portray the great tribulation period as a time of God's unbridled wrath. However, some have recognized that Christ actually attributed the flood of Noah's day to His post-tribulation return and not to the great tribulation. In an attempt to quickly recuperate, they quote from the book of Ezekiel that a day in prophecy represents a year and that Noah actually entered the ark seven days before the flood actually arrived. This would ultimately place the *rapture* of the church at the beginning of Daniel's seventieth week. This sounds compelling initially, but by reasoning in this manner, they are indirectly acknowledging that God's wrath will not occur throughout the great tribulation because again, the flood doesn't come until seven days *after* Noah enters the ark. If a day is representative of a year, then that would actually postpone God's wrath for seven years, placing it somewhere after the great tribulation period!

So which is it? Is God's wrath issued out during the great tribulation or isn't it? If they admit that it isn't, they lose enormous traction that the church is to be spared from the great tribulation because the whole theory hangs on whether God's wrath is issued out during that time. If they claim that the great tribulation is indeed a time of God's wrath, they not only directly oppose themselves because of the overlooked "seven days of silence," but they also directly oppose the very words of Christ who *clearly* and *strictly* categorized the flood with His post-tribulation descent from heaven.

Once again, this self-imposed contradiction brings to light the fallacies and dangers of this doctrine because while it may sound compelling from one angle, that angle *must* connect to all others to create the outline that the

Scriptures intended. If you try to establish doctrine based solely on one verse, one passage, or from an ad-hoc approach, you'll eventually (and probably quite quickly) be caught in other areas. Unfortunately, most believers aren't studied-up enough to see the overall outline, and therefore fall for rogue trinkets of misinformation.

Next to the confusion over I Thessalonians 5:9, I believe the incorrect application of the flood and its representation of God's wrath to the great tribulation to be the second most destructive inaccuracy that has many people deceived into believing that God's wrath will be unleashed during the great tribulation when, in fact, it cannot occur until after that time. This is confirmed by the confluence of Paul's letter, John's Revelation timelines, and Christ's prophecy which presents a single reoccurring theme: First the great tribulation, followed by the collection of the church, and *then* the wrath of God will ensue.

-*The Seven Vials*-

There are actually two distinctions to be made concerning the wrath that God will pour out in the future. Up to this point, I have focused heavily on the wrath that will occur on the day of the Lord; however, the first part of God's wrath will actually manifest in the form of the seven vials.

Revelation 15:7
*And one of the four beasts gave unto the **seven angels seven golden vials full of the wrath of God**, who liveth for ever and ever.*

The seven vials are essentially a warm-up to the second and most menacing part of the wrath that God will issue out on the day of the Lord. When do the seven vials begin and end? Again, if you recall, Revelation chapters 12-14 provide an accurate end time list which covers all of the significant events that are to occur at the end of this age, concluding with the battle of Armageddon. Therefore, it's a good possibility that if the seven vials don't occur after the battle of Armageddon, they are situated somewhere on that timeline. (Remember, Rev. 15-19 reverse gears chronologically and begin describing events laid out by the Rev. 12-14—only in further detail). To find out where the vials are located in the overall series of events is to simply take the terminology associated with the seven vials and compare it with the terminology offered on the Revelation 12-14 timeline. This permits an accurate assessment of where the vials are to be poured out in the overall grand scheme.

To give you a better understanding of what I'm talking about, Revelation chapter 15 starts out by depicting events that are to occur in heaven just prior to the pouring out of the first vial. It is in Revelation 15:4 that the saints surrounding the throne of God make a very important claim at that time:

Revelation 15:4
Who shall not fear thee, O Lord, and glorify thy name?
for thou only art holy: for all nations shall come and
worship before thee; ***for thy judgments are made***
manifest.

Prior to the pouring out of the first vial, we are told that God's judgments are—present tense—made manifest. The significance of this statement becomes evident when comparing this terminology against the latter part of the Revelation 12-14 timeline:

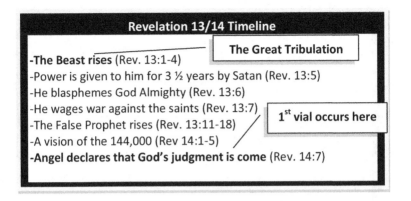

As you can see, the Revelation 12-14 timeline clearly mimics the terminology associated with the first vial. This gives an allowance to safely place the first vial of wrath at that particular juncture and provides the first major reliable indicator of when God actually begins to move in His fury. It is poured out *after* Satan's duration of power (the 42 months of the great tribulation period). This shows once again that God's wrath—no matter if it's in regards to the day of the Lord or to the vials of wrath—is to strictly occur as a post-tribulation event.

To determine when the seventh and final vial is poured out is to use the exact same technique. First, a look at the terminology provided at the seventh vial is needed.

Revelation 16:17,19
[17]And the seventh angel poured out his vial into the air;
*[19]...and great **Babylon** came in remembrance before God, to give unto her the cup of the **wine of the fierceness of his wrath**.*

Once again, the Revelation 13/14 timeline mimics this very terminology:

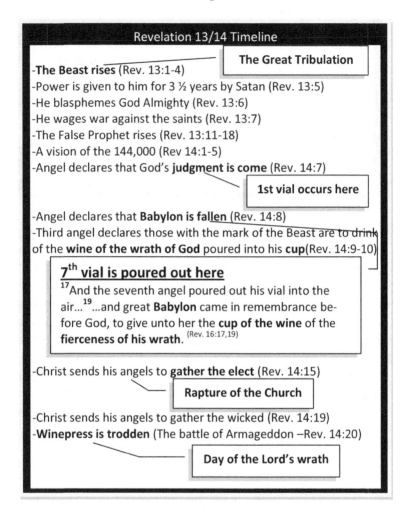

Revelation 13/14 Timeline

The Great Tribulation

-**The Beast rises** (Rev. 13:1-4)
-Power is given to him for 3 ½ years by Satan (Rev. 13:5)
-He blasphemes God Almighty (Rev. 13:6)
-He wages war against the saints (Rev. 13:7)
-The False Prophet rises (Rev. 13:11-18)
-A vision of the 144,000 (Rev 14:1-5)
-Angel declares that God's **judgment is come** (Rev. 14:7)

1st vial occurs here

-Angel declares that **Babylon is fallen** (Rev. 14:8)
-Third angel declares those with the mark of the Beast are to drink of the **wine of the wrath of God** poured into his **cup**(Rev. 14:9-10)

7th vial is poured out here

17And the seventh angel poured out his vial into the air…19…and great **Babylon** came in remembrance before God, to give unto her the **cup of the wine** of the **fierceness of his wrath**. (Rev. 16:17,19)

-Christ sends his angels to **gather the elect** (Rev. 14:15)

Rapture of the Church

-Christ sends his angels to gather the wicked (Rev. 14:19)
-**Winepress is trodden** (The battle of Armageddon –Rev. 14:20)

Day of the Lord's wrath

This information provides a great overall snapshot of how the entire end will unfold from the middle of Daniel's seventieth week onward. It also reveals that the judgment of God, seven vials of wrath, and the wrath of God that takes place at the battle of Armageddon on the day of the Lord *all* occur after the great tribulation.

Did you notice one other critical factor? The church *rapture* is listed after the seven vials! Since the church is not *raptured* until the day of the Lord, then the unnerving prospect presented before us is that the church will *still be here on earth* throughout the seven vials of wrath that God is to pour out. I am well aware that this information is sure to rock the boat, so I would like to quickly usher you to Revelation 16:14-16. These few verses are placed between the sixth and seventh vials.

> *Revelation 16:14-16*
> *14For they are the spirits of devils, working miracles, which go forth unto the kings of the earth and of the whole world, to gather them to the battle of that great day of God Almighty.*
> **15Behold, I come as a thief. Blessed is he that watcheth, and keepeth his garments, lest he walk naked, and they see his shame.**
> *16And he gathered them together into a place called in the Hebrew tongue Armageddon.*

This is an urgent reminder from God to the believers who are *still on earth* during the outpouring of the vials to watch for the soon-coming day of the Lord. But can this group of believers be identified specifically? The answer is yes because, first, there are multiple statements being made here that were instructions *originally given to the church* by Jesus Christ. The first two can be identified in association with the church of Sardis. In the first few chapters of Revelation, Christ, in addressing all seven churches, reminds the church of Sardis in Revelation chapter 3: "*If therefore thou shalt not watch, I will come on thee as a thief.*" The last one is found in association with the church of Laodicea in verse 18 of the same chapter: "*I counsel thee to buy of me gold tried in the fire, that thou mayest be rich; and white raiment, that thou mayest be clothed, and that the shame of thy nakedness do not appear."* It is apparent then that the verses found between the sixth and seventh vials are simply offering a reminder *originally given to the church* that all is soon to be fulfilled.

Furthermore, Paul is quite clear in his famous *rapture* passage to the Thessalonians, that the church *rapture* will not occur until the day of the Lord—a day that is now clearly being presented in the book of Revelation as one that will occur after the seven vials of wrath. This truth again leaves the church on earth throughout all seven vials.

-Revelation 3:10-

Since the church is indeed to be present on earth throughout the seven vials of wrath yet I Thessalonians 5:9 claims that we are not subject to the wrath of God, how is it possible for the church to be roaming the planet during that time? This is where the controversial 10th verse of Revelation 3 comes into the equation!

> Revelation 3:10
> *Because thou hast kept the word of my patience, I also will **keep thee from the hour of tempta-** **tion,** which shall come upon all the world, to try them that dwell upon the earth.*

Unfortunately, this verse has become a foundation in the pre-tribulation circle with claims that the word "keep" is an inference to the pre-tribulation *rapture* of the church and "the hour of temptation" is referring to Daniel's entire seventieth week. However, this interpretation is troublesome because to arrive at this conclusion, one must be subjective since no literal verification of these associations can be found elsewhere in Scripture. The strength of this claim is left more to opinion brought forth by those with preconceived ideas which is, quite frankly, dangerous.

To understand the true intent of this verse, a look at the Greek text is needed first. The Greek word for "temptation" is "peirasmos" which can also be defined as "trial." What is of particular interest is that this word is also utilized in the Greek Septuagint (The Greek version of the Old Testament) and can be found in the book of Deuteronomy.

 Deuteronomy 4:34
*Or hath God assayed to go and take him a nation from the midst of another nation, by **temptations**, by signs, and by wonders, and by war, and by a mighty hand, and by a stretched out arm, and by great terrors, according to all that the LORD your God did for you in Egypt before your eyes?*

Here, Moses offers a reminder to the children of Israel of how the Lord had delivered them from slavery out of the land of Egypt by diverse temptations (trials), signs, and wonders. This, of course, is referring to the ten plagues that came upon the Egyptians due to the hardness of Pharaoh's heart. Up to that point, the Israelites had suffered under immense hardships associated with the brutality of Egyptian slavery, but God hadn't forgotten about His chosen people and finally sent Moses—a Hebrew, raised Egyptian—to Pharaoh to convince him to relinquish the rights of the Israelites over to God. Pharaoh ultimately denies Him ten times and each time God sends the Egyptians a terrible plague of increasing intensity. These plagues were strictly limited to the Egyptians, their livestock, and their plots of land while the Israelites remained under supernatural protection. They were not only designed to convince a hard-hearted king of his error, but they were also designed to display the immensity of God's power.

However, the fact that Moses described the ten plagues of Egypt as "temptations" permits us to re-examine the controversial verse of Revelation 3:10, and reassess the "hour of temptation" as a possible reference—not to the great tribulation, but to an end time series of plagues that will be issued out on a worldwide scale. First, are there to be plagues poured out by God in this manner in the future?

Revelation 15:1
*And I saw another sign in heaven, great and marvell-ous, seven angels having the **seven last plagues**; for in them is filled up the wrath of God.*

These end time plagues are to come in the form of the *seven vials of wrath* that God will pour out just prior to the day of the Lord. However, this initial interrelationship between the ten plagues of Egypt, Revelation 3:10, and the seven vials of wrath doesn't stop there; it extends further with a reference back to the timeline of Revelation 13/14 I provided earlier on page 154. It is quite clear, when studying that timeline, that the seven last plagues are to occur between Revelation 14:7-8. This, in turn, provides another parallel between the seven vials of wrath, Revelation 3:10, and the account of the ten plagues in the Old Testament by considering the statement the angel makes just prior to the outpouring of the first plague/vial of wrath:

Revelation 14:17
*Fear God, and give glory to him; for the **hour of his judgment** is come:*

The coming seven plagues are considered by the angel to be the "hour of God's judgment." The significance of this statement becomes evident when considering that it was God Himself who referenced the same temptation (trial) of plagues Moses wrote about in the book of Deuteronomy as Godly *judgments* upon the land of Egypt:

> *Exodus 7:3-4*
> *3And I (God) will harden Pharaoh's heart, and multiply my signs and my wonders in the land of Egypt.*
> *4But Pharaoh shall not hearken unto you, that I may lay my hand upon Egypt, and bring forth mine armies, and my people the children of Israel, out of the land of Egypt by **great judgments.***

The truth is, the temptations of Egypt were recognized by God as judgments! When taking into consideration all the literal truths of God's Word as a whole, it becomes evident that the "hour of temptation" of Revelation 3:10 is actually to be recognized as an *hour of judgment*. This hour of judgment is located at Revelation 14:7 and, when correctly identifying the position of the seven vials on the end time timeline, is in relation to the *seven post-tribulation plagues*. Just as Revelation 3:10 reveals the coming temptation/judgment to be on worldwide scale, these plagues are to consume the entire planet and torment Satan's empire from the least to the greatest. Interestingly enough, they will be identical to some of the plagues originally unleashed upon Egypt.

Egyptian Plagues

River turns to blood, Boils on men, Hail, Darkness

Changed

Revelation Plagues

Sores on men, Sea/Rivers turn to blood, Darkness, Hail.

Christ's message to the church of Philadelphia in Revelation 3:10 is in reference to the *seven vials of wrath* that will be poured out *after* the great tribulation.

-"I Also Will Keep Thee"-

To answer the question of how God will "keep" the church (who will still be under the confines of mortality) from these seven coming plagues is to simply study how God protected the Israelites throughout the plagues unleashed upon the land of Egypt. *They were protected supernaturally.* God only asked one requirement of them in relation to the last plague which ended up taking the lives of every firstborn (including livestock) within Egypt's borders. To be exempt from this frightening event, the Israelites were instructed to slaughter a firstborn lamb without spot or blemish and cover the doorposts of their homes with its blood. As the angel of death went through Egypt that night, those with the covering were passed over and spared. The rest suffered the consequences. Thus, the feast of Passover was born and is still observed by orthodox Jews to this day.

Likewise, all who remain after the great tribulation, have denied the mark of the Beast, and have been obedient to God's Word will be considered God's chosen elect and, just like the Israelites, will be *kept* once more under God's wing and supernaturally protected in the very same manner as He, again, issues out His end time plagues that are to come in the form of the seven vials. Those with the testimony of Jesus—the sacrificial Lamb of the world—will have placed the blood of His sacrifice on the doorposts of their hearts through faith. When the seven vials of wrath are finally poured out, God will again *pass over* His elect, keeping them under His divine protection and judging only those outside the promises made to His people. In the end, whether it's supernatural protection on earth or resurrection and *rapture* salvation on the day of the Lord, in both scenarios, the true church of Christ will be protected from God's wrath.

-The Great Tribulation Defined-

Since the evidence is overwhelming that God's wrath is not unveiled until after the great tribulation, then the initial implications are that God will remain unmoved throughout that short period of time. If the great tribulation truly has no relationship to God's wrath, then what is its actual purpose? Fortunately, the Bible reveals that information!

Revelation 12,13
*12:12Woe to the inhabiters of the earth and of the sea! for the **devil is come down unto you, having great wrath**, because he knoweth that he hath but a short time.*
*12:14And to the woman were given two wings of a great eagle, that she might fly into the wilderness, into her place, where she is nourished **for a time, and times, and half a time**, (1+ 2 +1/2 equals 3.5 - great tribulation) from the face of the serpent.*
*12:17And the **dragon was wroth** with the woman, and **went to make war** with the remnant of her seed, which keep the commandments of God, and have the testimony of Jesus Christ*

*¹³:⁵And there was given unto him a mouth speaking great things and blasphemies; and power was given unto him to continue **forty and two months**. (great tribulation)*

¹³:⁶And he opened his mouth in blasphemy against God, to blaspheme his name, and his tabernacle, and them that dwell in heaven.

*¹³:⁷And it was given unto him to **make war** with the saints, and to **overcome them**: and power was given him over all kindreds, and tongues, and nations.*

What is the great tribulation about? *Satan's wrath!* Believers are quick to acknowledge and fear the wrath of God Almighty, but they forget that Satan has his own allotted time to pour out his own wrath. *That time consists of the great tribulation!* Satan is cast onto earth and realizes that he has but a short time left before he's ultimately condemned. He immediately directs his wrath against those with a testimony of Jesus Christ during this three and a half year great tribulation period.

With this understanding, small scriptural clues begin to appear that shows God is actually *waiting* during this time. The first and most prominent clue can be found in Revelation chapter 6:10. There, the fifth seal is opened which reveals all the Christian martyrs who were killed for their testimony and are now pleading under the altar of God.

Revelation 6:10
*And they cried with a loud voice, saying, How long, O Lord, holy and true, **dost thou NOT judge and avenge** our blood on them that dwell on the earth?*

162

It has already been previously determined from the listed celestial events contained within the sixth seal (a direct reference to Matthew 24:29) that the sixth seal occurs immediately after the great tribulation; so this question posed by the martyrs at the fifth seal *had to have been made during the great tribulation*. First, the Greek word used for judge here is "krino" (kree'-no). It means to avenge, conclude, condemn, damn, decree, determine, punish, or try. Essentially, the core question of the martyrs was this then: How long Lord are You going to _wait_ before pouring out Your wrath on the wicked? This makes verse 10 enormous in significance because it presents overwhelming evidence that God has *yet* to issue out His judgments, nor has He begun to avenge on behalf of His elect *even throughout the course of the great tribulation* according to the martyrs who are under the alter of God. These martyred believers were not incorrect in their assessment of God's wrathless demeanor during this time because they are told in the very next verse that their fellow servants must be killed *first* before God's wrath is finally released. This is an absolute foreign concept to any pre-tribulation believer yet made overly clear at the fifth seal.

Strangely, pre-tribulation proponents carry the idea that to suffer through the coming great tribulation period is to experience firsthand God's unrelenting anger. However, the question of the martyrs at the fifth seal actually firmly stands as a declaration of God's _silence_ during that time (in respect to His wrath). It clearly supersedes any insinuation that the great tribulation is a demonstration of His anger by revealing that God is actually _withholding_ His wrath during that time! To claim that the great tribulation is a time of God's wrath is to actually stand in direct opposition to the literal evidence found at the fifth seal which states to the contrary.

But even if this truth is completely ignored and the continued claim is that those who are finally converted to Christ within the great tribulation must now endure the wrath of God simply because of the poor timing in their spiritual decision making is *still* an outright contradiction of I Thessalonians 5:9 which states that believers are not appointed as such. Although some try to strictly tag the present day church with this promise, just a quick reflection on the days of Noah and of Lot—two righteous believers who lived thousands of years prior to the church age—reveals that both were spared from the wrath of God in each case. As a result, believers of *any era* are to receive the promise found in I Thessalonians 5:9 and that the so-called "tribulation saints" are *absolutely no exception* to this rule. Therefore, from the perspective of the pre-tribulation view, begs this question: If, through scriptural promises, the "tribulations saints" are *required* to be excluded from the wrath of God throughout the great tribulation, is there any legitimate reason to exclude the present day church from that time period?

-Who is like the Beast?-

Yet another clue of God's silence during the great tribulation in respect to His wrath appears in Revelation 13:4.

> *4And they (non-believers) worshipped the dragon (Satan) which gave power unto the beast: (Antichrist) and they worshipped the beast, saying, Who is like unto the beast? who is able to make war with him?*
> *5And there was given unto him a mouth speaking great things and blasphemies; and power was given*

*unto him to continue **forty and two months.*** (great tribulation)

Once again, the time period of these two verses is set in a strict great tribulation context where yet another question is found, and contains yet another underlying testimony to God's relationship to the great tribulation. This time, the question is made by the unbelievers instead of the martyrs. The collective question of the lost souls in allegiance to the Antichrist is this: Who is able to make war with this Beast? Of course, every believer knows the answer to that question: *God is able to make war with him.* However, the unbelievers during this great tribulation period are clearly only acknowledging the Beast as sole authority on earth at this point in time and obviously have not recognized God as entering into the war yet. Certainly, when God does begin to unleash His anger upon the inhabitants of the earth, it *will be* recognized by unbelievers as an unmistakable move of His Sovereign power (see Rev. 6:16). Yet curiously, those who are alive during the reign of the Antichrist seem to be totally oblivious to it according to Revelation 13:4! God's previous acts of wrath throughout Scripture have *never* been mistaken by humanity, so the only logical solution to this dilemma is that the reason the unbelievers are so captivated by the Antichrist and are posing such a blasphemous question during the great tribulation is simply because *God has yet to begin pouring out His wrath even up to this point.*

On the contrary, Scriptures make a clear presentation that, during this three and a half year period, Satan and his man of sin will have free reign without hindrance. They will have full global power and authority.

Revelation 13:7
*...and power was given him over **ALL** kindreds, and tongues, and nations.*

It should be considered that it would be extremely difficult for the forces of evil to exert this type of domination over the entire planet if truly suffering the wrath of God at the same time. It would also be ludicrous to think that God would use Satan as a conduit to pour out His own wrath for Him because He absolutely does not need Satan to do His bidding for Him. Furthermore, since the saints are overcome physically during the great tribulation, the end result would be a pouring out of God's wrath on His own church. That is absolutely contrary to His nature! We are separated and viewed righteous in Jesus Christ! God wouldn't bypass the Devil and persecute His own saints while Satan wallowed in his global power!

Even for God's wrath to be extended over a long time frame such as the three and half year great tribulation period is contrary to all His other previous acts of wrath throughout history. When Christ made references to the wrath of God, He used Noah's flood and Sodom and Gomorrah (Luke 17:26-33) as illustrations (both of which were in strict connection to His post-tribulation Second Coming in glory and not to the great tribulation). Even though the effects of the flood were seen for many years, the wicked were wiped out immediately; it was not dragged out for any extended period. Likewise, Sodom and Gomorrah suffered the same quick strike with the destruction of the city in a matter of minutes by fire. When God's wrath comes to fruition at the end of this age, *He will not deviate.* It will not trickle out, but will be a highly concentrated effort that will be over in rapid fire (See Zeph. 1:18).

These truths bring with it the realization that the great tribulation is set aside for Satan who will grasp the world in his evil grip by working through his man of sin. He will take advantage of this new found power by coming against the Jewish people and the true church with great wrath, but his wrath will pale in comparison to the rebuttal God will finally give him after the great tribulation is over. Again and again, Scripture flows seamlessly and in unison, providing the evidence for a strict post-tribulation move of God in His righteous anger against those who are not His own while the believers are fully protected. For once the great tribulation has run its short course, God will then rise up in His fury to make the whole earth tremble, and the time of Satan's kingdom and short reign here on earth will come to an abrupt end.

The Imminence Returned

I've heard many preachers over the years make the statement that at any moment the *rapture* could occur. "Are you ready?" they exclaim as they click their fingers to illustrate the instantaneous transformation; "or will you be left behind!" The crowd is deathly quiet. Somewhere in the congregation, a baby begins crying as if God had poked him in his little ribs to set the atmosphere. While the idea of an imminent *rapture* is an exciting notion and an introspective moment, how much truth is there to this statement?

This concept, whether realized or not, has its beginning in Matthew 24 and is based on a combination of statements made by Christ—first in verse 36—that "no man knows the day or the hour." This is followed by the thief-in-the-night analogy found a few verses later. The claim made on behalf is that no further prophecy needs to be fulfilled presently in order for Christ to return, allowing for an any-second coming.

Certainly at face value, a case could be built around

these few verses for an imminent return, but a closer look reveals that Christ was actually inferring something to the contrary. The truth is, when you begin to study these verses within the confines of the passage, it becomes immediately apparent that Christ was strictly speaking of His post-tribulation coming with all power and glory and not a pre-tribulation return.

> *Matthew 24:29-31,36,43*
> *29**Immediately after the tribulation** of those days shall the sun be darkened, and the moon shall not give her light, and the stars shall fall from heaven, and the powers of the heavens shall be shaken:*
> *30And then shall appear the sign of the Son of man in heaven: and then shall all the tribes of the earth mourn, and they shall see the **Son of man coming** in the clouds of heaven with power and great glory.*
> *31And he shall send his angels with a great sound of a trumpet, and they shall **gather together his elect** from the four winds, from one end of heaven to the other.*
> *36**But of that day and hour knoweth no man, no, not the angels of heaven, but my Father only.***
> *43But know this, that if the goodman of the house had known in what watch **the thief** would come, he would have watched, and would not have suffered his house to be broken up.*

On the one hand, Jesus was very specific about the timing of His return, telling His disciples that He will descend in the clouds of heaven immediately after the great tribulation. Almost in the same breath, however, He makes another interesting claim: *"But of that day and hour knoweth no man."* What did He mean by this? He's going to return immediately after the great tribulation, but no man knows the day or the hour? How could He be so specific in one instance but slap an unspecific label on it in the next? There are only two possible solutions. The first solution is that Jesus had completely overlooked the fact that He had just given His disciples a specific post-tribulation timeframe, instead, changing His mind a few verses later that His return would actually be fully imminent as soon as His feet left the Mount of Olives in His ascension back to heaven. The second solution is that His return is at least contingent upon the fulfillment of the great tribulation period and *then,* no man knows the exact day or hour of His return. Taking into consideration the actual context surrounding verse 36 (a must if you want to extract the truth), it becomes quickly apparent that Jesus was speaking about the latter.

In truth, Jesus had already made it fully apparent which day He was talking about when He said "But of *that* day." That day? Which day Lord? A pre-tribulation day? *On the contrary.* The only day that Christ had fully described to His disciples up to that point, and the day that can be found sitting just a few verses above verse 36 *is the day that Christ descends after the great tribulation.* Christ was actually pointing His readers to His post-tribulation return when He said *"that day!"* This reveals that no man knows the day or the hour of His return, but that *His return is at least conditional upon the complete fulfillment of the great tribulation first.* This is a major clue to genuine watchers!

How then, can the doctrine of an imminent pre-tribulation return be built around verses 36 and 43 when Jesus was in strict context with His post-tribulation descent from heaven to earth when He made those statements? There's no legitimate way unless, of course, these few verses are ripped out of context. You would have to steal verses 36 and 43 from Matthew 24, completely sever its original meaning, and plop it down into a context of your own creation to make it work. *Unfortunately, this is exactly what the pre-tribulation rapture theory does.* In doing so, however, it steps into uncharted territory that is not backed by Scripture.

The truth is, it's actually impossible to claim that Christ could return at any given second based on these few verses because Jesus strictly connected them to His return in glory *after* the great tribulation. Since we have not experienced the great tribulation yet, then the initial implications are that additional prophecy must be fulfilled before Christ can return, rendering an imminent return impossible at this present moment. This is undoubtedly a hard pill to swallow for any pre-tribulation theorist and is probably one of the biggest reasons why the post-tribulation viewpoint is rejected.

-*Like A Thief In The Night*-

Perhaps the most widely utilized concept in promoting an imminent return of Jesus Christ is the thief-in-the-night imagery which has infiltrated the psyche of the modern church and convinced millions that Jesus could return at any moment. However, a dissection of Christ's thief analogy reveals many important factors which begin to surface upon deeper investigation. For example, Christ reminds the church of Sardis:

Revelation 3:3
*Remember therefore how thou hast received and heard, and hold fast, and repent. If therefore thou shalt **not watch**, I will come on thee as a **thief**, and*

thou shalt not know what hour I will come upon thee.

Here, Christ uses the famous thief analogy once more but states: Watch <u>or</u> I will come on you as a thief. For most, this significance goes without any notice, but it's a crucial statement because it begins to draw a line between two groups of people:

1) Those who *aren't* watching.
2) Those who *are* watching.

Returning to Matthew 24, Christ begins explaining this separation in more detail and reveals exactly how each group will be affected by His return. He uses Noah as an example to help illustrate His point better.

Matthew 24:37-38
37But as the days of Noah were, so shall also the coming of the Son of man be.
*38For as in the days that were before the flood **they** were eating and drinking, marrying and giving in marriage, until the day that Noe entered into the ark,*

Here, Christ specifically lists and identifies the two separate groups:

1) <u>*They*</u> were eating, drinking and marrying (non-believers).
2) Until the day that Noah entered into the ark (believers).

Then in Matthew 24:39, He makes the following statement:

Matthew 24:39
*And knew not until the flood came, and took **them***
all away; so shall also the coming of the Son of man
be.

Jesus concentrates on the non-believers first. The flood
took *them* all away. Even though *they* were repeatedly
warned by Noah and his family, *they* just laughed him off
as a crazy old man with a half built boat in his back yard.
They ended up being taken by surprise in the end—*like a*
thief in the night. But will Christ come suddenly upon His
elect in this fashion like He does with the unbeliever? It's
immediately addressed:

Matthew 24:43
But know this, that if the goodman of the house had
*known in what watch the **THIEF** would come, he*
*would have **watched**, and would **not have suf-***
fered his house to be broken up.

Upon likening His return to the days of Noah, Christ
concluded with this infamous thief analogy that has, unfortunately, been taken out of context by so many teachers in
the church today and abused doctrinally. However, careful
reading of this statement reveals three crucial points. First,
in contrast to much of the jargon being spewed from today's pulpits, Christ indirectly tells His disciples that those
who are genuinely watching for His return will *not* be overtaken like a thief. Second, the "goodman" of the house (the
believer/watcher) will actually know in what watch the
thief (Christ) is coming. Third, the believer/watcher will

know this information because Christ was in context with His post-tribulation return when He made that statement (rendering a pre-tribulation application to this verse fully unscriptural).

Amazingly, the pre-tribulation *rapture* theory takes all three of these obvious points of Matthew 24:43 and completely flips them upside down: Christ will come before the tribulation upon His own church suddenly (the goodman) because the church has absolutely no idea when the Lord is coming!

Christ specifically used Noah as an illustration because He wanted today's believers to make all the right connections. As Matthew 24:43 states, Noah (the goodman) *was not* overtaken by the massive worldwide flood. He was a believer acting upon his faith with preparation all while watching. Noah knew it was on the horizon and was preparing and watching for it in advance because God specifically warned him of the impending danger coming upon the wicked and gave him explicit instructions each step of the way on how to prepare for God's coming interaction with humanity. Noah did what was instructed of him and, in the end, his life was spared when God supernaturally shut him in the ark and took him away.

Just as God gave Noah specific instructions in his day, Christ does for every believer in this era—presented in His essential prophecy of Matthew 24. Once more, Jesus warns the righteous followers of God of the disaster coming from above upon a lost humanity when He returns (after the tribulation according to His own words). Once more, He compels His believers to prepare and watch for the signs, and once more, provides a specific timing of when the righteous should expect to be taken away in salvation (see Matt. 24:29-31).

As a result, the combination of Matthew 24:43 and Christ's example of Noah produces the same conclusion each time: *The day that Christ returns will <u>not</u> overtake the believer (watcher) like a thief!* The truth is, the return of Jesus Christ is only imminent, and will only come like a thief in the night to *<u>those who aren't watching</u>*. Furthermore, believers *will actually know* in what season the Lord is coming because of all the specifics listed in Matthew 24. This is exactly why Jesus used the analogy of the fig tree to describe His return: *Now learn a parable of the fig tree; When his branch is yet tender, and putteth forth leaves, ye know that summer is nigh* (vs. 32). Jesus specifically used the illustration of seasons because He was making a point to believers everywhere that knowing the season is not optional, but is *required* for every person who wishes to be a part of God's end time salvation plan on the day of His wrath—*just as it was in the days of Noah.*

But when is the day of His wrath? As discussed in a previous chapter, Noah's flood is indeed a clear symbol of God's wrath; however, Christ unmistakably parallels the flood of Noah's day to His Second Coming in glory *after* the great tribulation and not to the great tribulation period itself. Pre-tribulation advocates love to use the flood to try to prove a pre-tribulation *rapture* of the church. The problem is, they erroneously apply the symbol of the flood to what they deem the tribulation period (the last seven years) because they think that this is the time when God begins pouring out His wrath. However, Christ makes absolutely no correlation between the tribulation period and Noah's flood throughout His *entire* discourse of Matthew 24. Instead, Jesus specifically attributed the flood to the day He is revealed—a day He clearly stated would occur immediately after the tribulation (Matthew 24:29-39). *In truth, the symbol of the flood has nothing to do with the great tribulation at all.* It's all in strict reference to the Second

Coming of Christ after that time. In relation, the application of Noah's flood to anything other than the post-tribulation return of Christ has absolutely no scriptural basis, and directly conflicts with the very words of Jesus. Really, from the perspective of the pre-tribulation view, the flood symbol must be shifted seven years down the road and applied to the day of the Lord for the sake of truth preservation.

What *can* be applied to the great tribulation from the story of Noah was his preparation. If Noah didn't prepare for what was ahead, he too would have been washed away with the rest of the world. His preparation involved building an ark; he was building a safe haven. He suffered ridicule and persecution during that time but pressed forward because he was more concerned about watching for God's promise of total annihilation (and his salvation) rather than worldly tribulation. Pre-tribulation advocates are too "caught up" with escaping tribulation when, truthfully, they should be focusing on getting prepared for the Lord's return after that time. As individuals, we must be presently building our own safe haven. That haven is Jesus Christ. We must build and strengthen our relationship with Him so that we can endure worldly persecutions and tribulations all while keeping a watchful eye for God's promise of return in fiery vengeance (and our salvation). If we don't, we too will be washed away in the wake of chaos that is soon to overcome this planet when He returns.

-II Peter 3:10-

In II Peter 3, the apostle Peter wrote his second letter to the early church and, like Jesus, also used the thief imagery:

II Peter 3:10
*But the day of the Lord will come as a **thief in the
night**;*

Interestingly, Peter doesn't associate the thief phrase
with Christ's coming specifically but instead, attaches it to
the coming day of the Lord—a day discussed in vivid detail
all throughout the Old Testament. Why did Peter make it a
point to utilize the same thief imagery used by Christ in
Matthew 24, but attach it to the Old Testament day of the
Lord instead? Pre-tribulation believers would immediately
intervene here and claim it's because both days are to come
in the same manner, but that both days are to occur on
separate occasions. If it could be proven, however, that the
day of the Lord has a clear stake in Matthew 24, couldn't it
be assumed that Peter was pointing towards that particular
chapter and Christ's post-tribulation return instead of to
some random Old Testament passage? Excluding the evident thief reference used by both Jesus and Peter, are their
passages connected further and if so, where? The answer
rests in Matthew 24:29. Though Christ was specifically divulging information about His own return there, He also
includes a vivid description about the complete darkening
of the sun, moon, and stars (Matt. 24:29)—an event *clearly
tied* to the day of the Lord and described in numerous
chapters and verses throughout the Old Testament (see
Isaiah 13:9-10, Joel 2:31 & Joel 3:14-15). This evidence reveals that the day of the Lord does have a distinct part in
Matthew 24, and Christ's return, being disclosed at the
same time, is scripturally interchangeable with that term.

But yet another parallel can be found. Just as Jesus li-
kened His return to the days of Noah, so does Peter remind
the early church of Noah's flood in relation to the coming
day of the Lord: *Whereby the world that then was, being*

overflowed with water, perished (vs. 6). It's clear then, that Peter, in his second letter to the present day church, was actually gleaning from Christ's prophecy of Matthew 24—evident from the three clear connecters found between the two passages (the thief imagery, the day of the Lord references, and the Noah comparisons).

Even though Peter used an Old Testament term in his letter, he actually had Jesus Christ's post-tribulation return in mind when he used it because he fully understood that Christ was indirectly speaking about the Old Testament day of the Lord when describing His own return in Matthew 24 (and so did the early church apparently).

Outside of the stringent and evident post-tribulation restrictions placed on the thief imagery in Matthew 24:43 when interpreting within the confines of context, Peter's use of the thief metaphor in relation to the day of the Lord—a day that is also clearly connected to the twenty fourth chapter of Matthew—is also strictly post-tribulation in occurrence and shows that no pre-tribulation insinuation can be found in II Peter 3 either.

-*More Confirmation Through Revelation*-

The thief-in-the-night statement is also found in Revelation 16:15 and offers up even more evidence on how it is to be interpreted.

Revelation 16:13-16
13And I saw three unclean spirits like frogs come out of the mouth of the dragon, and out of the mouth of the beast, and out of the mouth of the false prophet.
14For they are the spirits of devils, working miracles, which go forth unto the kings of the earth and

*of the whole world, to gather them to the battle of that great **day of God** Almighty.*

*¹⁵**Behold, I come as a thief**. Blessed is he that watcheth, and keepeth his garments, lest he walk naked, and they see his shame.*

¹⁶And he gathered them together into a place called in the Hebrew tongue Armageddon.

Even pre-tribulation proponents will agree that the setting of these few verses strictly concerns the coming battle of Armageddon—that last great apocalyptic war between the forces of good and evil when Jesus returns on the day of the Lord. It is here, that the Bible strictly correlates the thief imagery with the post-tribulation day of the Lord *for a third time*.

Interestingly, the Scofield Study Bible, like many other editions, uses red letters to identify when Christ is speaking yet deemed "behold, I come as a thief" to be a statement spoken by someone other than Jesus Christ and leaves the lettering in black. Certainly, if I was a pre-tribulation *rapture* theory pioneer such as Scofield was, I wouldn't want the church to know that it's actually Christ Himself offering this final warning here in strict context with the post-tribulation day of God either! This would only further prove that Christ was indeed connecting the thief imagery of Matthew 24:43 strictly to His post-tribulation coming because it's exactly what He does here in the book of Revelation. However, the truth is, *it was* Christ speaking here because it was *His* revelation to John.

But if Christ was actually inferring an imminent pre-tribulation *rapture* of the church by way of the thief analogy in Matthew 24 (which He clearly isn't), then why is this statement reused in the book of Revelation at a juncture that is clearly post-tribulation in nature? The answer is that

Revelation 16:15 is simply mimicking Matthew 24:43—both in terminology and context. It validates that the thief analogy is to be strictly interpreted in a post-tribulation manner and that it has absolutely nothing to do with an imminent pre-tribulation *rapture* whatsoever. Where is the pre-tribulation insinuation to be found in Scripture in relation to the thief imagery? The answer is: *It can't be found anywhere!* The only way to imply an imminent pre-tribulation return would be to, again, rip all of these mentioned texts out of context and apply them to a doctrine of your own making.

-*Paul's Parallel*-

As always, Paul summed up very nicely in I Thessalonians what Christ revealed to His disciples in Matthew 24 and later to John in his revelation.

I Thessalonians 5:2
*For yourselves know perfectly that the day of the Lord so cometh as a **thief in the night.***

Just as Peter used the thief imagery in relation to the day of the Lord, so did the apostle Paul in his first letter to the Thessalonians. *Yet again,* this specific illustration is encountered in strict conjunction with the post-tribulation day of the Lord. For a *fourth time,* the Bible confirms that this correlation is to be interpreted in a strict post-tribulation timeframe.

Similarly, Paul immediately began separating the two groups just as Christ did in Matthew 24.

I Thessalonians 5:3
*For when **they** shall say, Peace and safety; then sudden destruction cometh upon them, as travail upon a woman with child; and they shall not escape.*

For when *they*....who is "they"? It is all those who are *not* watching for Jesus Christ's return—the nonbelievers. *They* will be in their sin, worshipping the Beast, and wearing his mark in submission to his system so as to avoid persecution and death. All will seemingly be peaceful for *them,* oblivious to the sudden destruction that will overcome *them* when Christ returns on the day of the Lord. But Paul immediately reassures the believers:

I Thessalonians 5:4,6
⁴But ye, brethren, are not in darkness, that that day should overtake you as a thief.
⁶*Therefore let us not sleep, as do others; but let us* **watch** *and be sober.*

This verse is crucial in determining the truth because even though Christ was somewhat cryptic in Matthew 24:43 about the thief, Paul takes it and spells it right out for the church, making it absolutely undeniable: *Those who are watching (believers) for that day (day of Christ/day of the Lord) will <u>NOT</u> be overtaken like a thief in the night.* Verse 4 not only corrects the erroneous association between the thief-in-the-night analogy and a pre-tribulation *rapture* of the church by applying it to the post-tribulation day of the Lord once more, it also negates the believer from experiencing an imminent thief-in-the-night return by Christ at all. Why? Because we will be watching unlike the rest of the world! Again the truth remains: *The return of Jesus Christ is only imminent for those who aren't watching!*

An obvious error in the pre-tribulation *rapture* doctrine immediately comes to the surface in light of this important information. It's found in their repeated attempts to impose an imminent thief-in-the-night return by Christ—not only on the unbelievers—*but on the believers as well,* all while trying to do so in a pre-tribulation context. This notion violates the Scriptures! Nowhere does it indicate that believers (watchers) are to be overtaken like a thief, and nowhere can the pre-tribulation suggestion be found. This line of thought completely ignores what Christ and Paul were actually trying to communicate to the elect.

The next time you hear a preacher claim that Christ will overtake His church like a thief in the night, you might want to gently remind him that he's actually implying his entire congregation is unsaved! True believers will be watching and will not be overtaken in this fashion.

-*Watchers Field Manual*-

Since believers are commanded to watch, then it is imperative we understand what it is we are to be watching for. Fortunately, the Bible presents many of the preceding events, allowing watchers to be in-the-know. In II Thessalonians 2:2, Paul made it clear that the day of Christ is to be preceded by a falling away apostasy and the rise of the Antichrist—events that have yet to be fulfilled in their entirety and that must come to pass before Christ can return. Just reading that passage strictly in its most basic literal sense destroys the idea of an imminent return. While I know that many claim that this particular day of Christ is to be interpreted separately from the *rapture* of the church, there are no arguments that this day *should be* connected to Matthew 24—the day that Christ descends after the great tribulation on the day of the Lord to punish the wicked.

However, isn't this where the doctrine of an any-second imminent return was strangely birthed? Truly, if the two passages are to be connected together, then nothing is to be omitted which means that no man knows the day or the hour of Christ's day of II Thessalonians 2:2 either. Yet Paul was bold enough to state that a falling away apostasy and the rise of the Antichrist is *still* to precede that day.

Christ would have not admonished Paul for his boldness because *even Jesus* admitted that He doesn't know the exact day or hour that He will descend (only the Father knows), and yet He too boldly declared that a great tribulation must still come first.

When placing these two passages together, the idea of an imminent return in any broad sense gets quickly lost and is refined down to a very tiny window which is dependent upon a specific series of events that must precede it before it becomes plausible. Christ's return will only become truly imminent once the falling away has come to its completion, *only once* the Antichrist has risen to power, and *only once* the great tribulation has performed its prophetic duties. Even then, true believers will still not be overtaken like a thief because if they have managed to escape all those things and have been accounted worthy enough to make it to that point, they will now be following Paul's instruction in I Thessalonians 5:6 to be watching for the day of the Lord with an unmatched sense of urgency. Paul placed that instruction there because he knew any basic student of Scripture would realize that before the day of the Lord can come, the sun, moon, and stars will literally be darkened (Joel 2:31)—the last yet principal sign of Christ's appearing. When this supernatural event finally unfolds overhead after the great tribulation (Matthew 24:29), true watchers will know exactly what's going on and understand its monumental significance. They'll realize that the return of Christ is *now* finally at hand and will lift their heads (and probably their hands!) to the skies in unparalleled anticipation, obsessively scanning the darkened heavens and watching for what couldn't have taken place ever before in human history, but *now* could occur at any given second. In contrast, unbelievers will still be in total subjection to the Antichrist at that point and will be completely oblivious to what's about to come upon them *like a thief*.

-*More Preceding Signs*-

In Matthew 24, Christ also provided a detailed list of additional signs that will precede this supernatural celestial event and His return in glory. Just glance at this list and you soon realize how close we really are to the end of all things. We stand at the threshold of the Antichrist's appearance! Once he appears, it will be a snowball effect of exponential intensity that in a matter of only a few years, will be destroyed by the power of Jesus Christ's return!

Preceding Signs
• **Deceivers**
• **False christs**
• **Wars and rumors of wars**
• **Famine**
• **Pestilence**
• **Earthquakes in diverse places**
• **Christian martyrdom**
• **False prophets**
• **Overwhelming sin**
• **Lack of natural affection in man**
• **The abomination of desolation** *(The Antichrist abolishes the daily sacrifices and stands in the temple demanding sole worship)*
• **Shortened days**
• **A time of great tribulation**
• **Sun/moon/stars darkened**

Christ reminds us in Matthew 24:33 and also in the book of Luke:

Matthew 24:33
So likewise ye, when ye shall see all these things, know that it (Second Coming) is near, even at the doors.
Luke 21:28
And when these things begin to come to pass, then look up, and lift up your heads; for your redemption draweth nigh

-Daniel's Addition-

The book of Daniel offers yet another important clue to the list. At the end of his vision, Daniel asks the angel how long it will be to the end of all the things that were shown to him.

Daniel 12:11
*And from the time that the daily sacrifice shall be taken away, and the abomination that maketh desolate set up, there shall be a **thousand two hundred and ninety days**.*

The angel informs Daniel that once the Antichrist abolishes the daily sacrifices (the abomination of desolation), there will only be 1260 days plus another 30 days remaining. But wait a minute...if we aren't supposed to know the day or the hour, doesn't this verse tell us exactly when Christ will return? Not so. The angel then adds:

Daniel 12:12
Blessed is he that waiteth, and cometh to the thou-
sand three hundred and five and thirty days.

There is an additional 45 days given. It's not mentioned what will occur here, however, it's *highly probable* that Christ will return between this time, and whoever comes to the 1335 days is considered "blessed." They are considered blessed at this point because they will have now entered into the new era of the millennial kingdom. No man knows the day or the hour of Christ's return; however, Daniel's passage is truly exciting because it gives those of under-standing (the watchers) a real possibility of calculating to within a *month and a half* of Christ's actual Second Com-ing! This is how we will know in what watch the thief will come! (Matt. 24:43.)

This statement is sure to ruffle the feathers of many be-cause, for so long, the church has been inundated with the teaching that Christ's return could occur at absolutely any moment. This is further overshadowed by the school of thought that actually calculating the *rapture* timing and Christ's return, whether it is within a month and half or 10 ½ years is taboo. What has to be re-considered is that even if you believe in an escapist's *rapture*—an ideology that ab-solutely prohibits its followers from pinpointing any type of date range, the truth of Christ's "re-return" within this par-ticular 45 day window of opportunity *remains absolutely legitimate scripturally* for all those who find themselves in the great tribulation. When the abomination of desolation spoken of by the prophet Daniel is set up, the prophetic countdown will begin no matter if you were "pre," "mid," "post," or anything in between and believers who are thrust into that time period will be making these very calcula-tions. This shows that isolating a particular timeframe for

Christ's return is not as taboo as one might have originally thought. It's merely a question of which group will find themselves in the middle of it all—checking off each day like chalk on a concrete jail wall. Will it be the church or will it be the lonely tribulation saints? Obviously, pre-tribulation advocates claim exemption, but I believe I have already presented enough evidence in this book to the contrary, revealing that this 45 day window to glory is for the present day church.

-A Closer Look-

Again, Christ hinted to the fact that true believers will actually know in what watch the thief will come. Since the church will indeed find itself within the great tribulation period, then understanding how time will operate during this short span is crucial so that we are not left in the dark (no pun intended) and uneducated about the general time of Christ's arrival. Life will not be easy during this period, so having an idea of how long it will continue will become of utmost importance. The hope of glory may be the only thing to cling to during this time! Again, contrary to popular belief, Scriptures unveil many important clues that condense Christ's possible day of arrival down to a very small fragment of time.

As revealed in a previous chapter, the great tribulation will be 1260 days in length (Revelation 11). Scripture also reveals that the days of the great tribulation will literally be shortened to eight hour intervals (4th trumpet). That's 1260 days at 8 hours a day. Christ tells us that the great tribulation will begin when we see the abomination of desolation set up by the Antichrist, revealing that we should begin counting the 1260 days on that particular day. Daniel states that the end will then come 1290 days after the abomination of desolation, indicating an additional 30 day increment. Referring back to the "Operation of Revelation" chart I provided on pages 106-107, it becomes immediately apparent that this 30 day period is specifically set aside for the unleashing of the seven vials of wrath upon the earth just prior to the day of the Lord. Taking this into consideration, when the first vial is unleashed, grievous sores will come upon all those who had worshipped the Antichrist, signifying to the watchers that they have now crossed over the great tribulation finish line and that God is finally beginning to intervene on their behalf. In the middle of this 30 day period, God will turn off the celestial lights—a sixth seal/fifth vial combination—fulfilling Christ's prophecy of Matthew 24:29 with total accuracy. The completion of the seven vials within this 30 day period will be followed by the last 45 day interval (blessed is he that comes to the 1335 days) of continued around-the-clock darkness. Understand that it will become increasingly difficult to keep track of which day it actually is during this full blackout of the heavens because it's not mentioned if God returns to counting a day as a normal 24 hour period, or if He continues with the eight hour increments such as it was during the great tribulation. Furthermore, suffering through a series of completely darkened days will surely be disorientating in itself! As it is written: "no man knows the _day_ or the _hour_."

However, it is _somewhere_ during this 45 day increment that the unmatchable and paramount sign of glory that Christ prophesied about in Matthew 24, and that true believers have been so desperately waiting and watching for throughout the great tribulation period, will _finally_ protrude through the darkness of that day. This light will shine forth with blinding brilliance and in immensely supreme power as Jesus Christ—Name above all names—descends from the heavens on a cloud with a shout. Following Him

will be an innumerable mixture of both angels and heavenly saints and the reverberating sound of that last ear-
piercing trumpet blast which will resonate through the soul
of every man or woman—either with great joy or with great
fear. This magnificent and unparalleled event will finally
initiate the catching away of the church, and the battle of
Armageddon will ensue.

Satan's fingerprints can clearly be seen all over the pre-
tribulation theory at this advent of important information
because, as you can see, carrying around this kind of knowledge would steer you away from deception that will reign
supreme during his final rampage, give you a decisive
watcher's list, and an unwavering hope of soon coming salvation. Unfortunately, the pre-tribulation theory curiously
declares that Christ will overtake His church like a thief in
the night before she ever finds herself in a position to be
watching for this particular day of the Lord—leaving her in
an *extremely* vulnerable position. In just a few short conversations, it is easy to recognize that most who are placing
their hope in an escapist *rapture* are truly ignorant concerning the great tribulation period because of their exemption list mentality. Unfortunately, without realizing it,
they have *already* fallen victim to the lies of the Devil and
will be blindsided at the most inopportune moment. If, before the race starts, you find yourself tied to the gate, how
do you expect to cross the finish line? Remember, Jesus
stated that deception will be so rampant at that time that, if
it were possible, it would even deceive the very elect of
God! In fact, the first warning out of Christ's mouth concerning the time of the end was: "Take heed that no man
deceive you" (Matthew 24:4). The truth is, if you are already deceived by the time real deception comes, it's unlikely that you'll ever awaken to the truth when it really
matters. Deception is an area I personally want to avoid at

all cost. It should be your prayer too.

I earnestly pray that the Holy Spirit will bring to remembrance all of this critical information at its appointed time, and keep all who are truly watching for the Lord's return safe from the clutches of the adversary. Through Jesus' Name I pray to you Father, Amen.

Mark 13:37
And what I say unto you I say unto all, **Watch**

Separation of Church and State

When Christ shed His blood on the cross, the Mosaic Law was dissolved and a new covenant was established, ushering in a new era or dispensation that now included the salvation of the Gentiles.

Galatians 3:13-14
13Christ hath redeemed us from the curse of the law, being made a curse for us: for it is written, Cursed is every one that hangeth on a tree:
14That the blessing of Abraham might come on the Gentiles through Jesus Christ; that we might receive the promise of the Spirit through faith.

Those of non-Jewish descent, who choose to place their trust in Christ for salvation become Abraham's seed—not by bloodline—but by faith.

Galatians 3:26-29
26For ye are all the children of God by faith in Christ Jesus.
27For as many of you as have been baptized into Christ have put on Christ.
28There is neither Jew nor Greek, there is neither bond nor free, there is neither male nor female: for ye are all one in Christ Jesus.
29And if ye be Christ's, then are ye Abraham's seed, and heirs according to the promise.

Our faith in Christ allows us to now partake of the promises made to Abraham thousands of years ago (I'm speaking from the perspective of a Gentile). Faith has always been God's agenda from the start. Abraham, who fathered the nation of Israel, originally operated in faith and was not under the Mosaic Law. It wasn't till over 400 years later that the law came into existence. Its main purpose was to teach us that we can never obtain enough righteousness on our own to be accounted worthy in the sight of God. When Christ fulfilled the law and became the perfect sacrifice, we were then able to set our hope and faith on Him to be counted worthy to enter the Kingdom of God.

Unfortunately, the Jews became so enamored with their own workings of the law, they became blind to the concept of faith—the work of Christ on the cross being incomprehensible. This caused them to reject the new covenant and remain in the old.

Romans 9:31-33
31But Israel, which followed after the law of righteousness, hath not attained to the law of righteousness.

*32Wherefore? Because they sought it not by faith, but
as it were by the works of the law. For they stumbled
at that stumblingstone;*
*33As it is written, Behold, I lay in Sion a stumbling-
stone and rock of offence: and whosoever believeth
on him shall not be ashamed.*

Christ became a stumbling block to Israel which led
them into a nationalized blindness from the truth of the
gospel. However, through their fall came an opportunity for
the rest of the nations. Fortunately, God, in His mighty
wisdom, foresaw the rejection of the Messiah ahead of
time. He used it to bring in a new era, coaxing the Gentiles
into the fold to partake in the blessings initially meant for
Israel to provoke non-believing Israel to jealousy so that
they might ultimately return to Christ.

Romans 11:11
*I say then, Have they (Israel) stumbled that they
should fall? God forbid: but rather through their fall
salvation is come unto the Gentiles, for to provoke
them to jealousy.*

The apostles didn't understand this concept at the time
because when they finally realized Jesus had risen from the
grave, they assumed Christ would immediately crush all
rule and authority in Israel and proclaim His true position
of power at that time.

Acts 1:6
*...Lord, wilt thou at this time restore again the king-
dom to Israel?*

Christ tells them in verse 7:

...It is not for you to know the times or the seasons,
which the Father hath put in his own power

Later, Paul finally uncovered the mystery of this delay by revelation of God, and relays the information in a letter to the Ephesians.

Ephesians 3:3,5-6
3How that by revelation he made known unto me the mystery;
5Which in other ages was not made known unto the sons of men, as it is now revealed unto his holy apostles and prophets by the Spirit;
6That the Gentiles should be fellowheirs, and of the same body, and partakers of his promise in Christ by the gospel:

The mystery that had not made known previously, but was now made know to the apostle Paul, was a new era, set aside to incorporate the Gentiles into the church. Praise God! This era has come to be known as the dispensation of grace—a concept verified by Paul in Ephesians 3:2. It is a time period associated with the church that most agree, began with Israel's rejection of Christ, His crucifixion, and the day of Pentecost. However, the controversy lies not in when this current dispensation began so much as when it *ends.* Those of the pre-tribulation *rapture* persuasion believe that it will end before Daniel's seventieth week unfolds, followed by a reversion by God back to the old Mosaic Law dispensation throughout the last seven years to readdress the nation of Israel and the Jewish people specifically. To understand this concept with more clarity, a look at Daniel's prophecy of chapter nine is warranted.

Daniel 9:24-27

24Seventy weeks are determined upon thy people and upon thy holy city, to finish the transgression, and to make an end of sins, and to make reconciliation for iniquity, and to bring in everlasting righteousness, and to seal up the vision and prophecy, and to anoint the most Holy.

25Know therefore and understand, that from the going forth of the commandment to restore and to build Jerusalem unto the Messiah the Prince shall be seven weeks, and threescore and two weeks: the street shall be built again, and the wall, even in troublous times.

26And after threescore and two weeks shall Messiah be cut off, but not for himself: and the people of the prince that shall come shall destroy the city and the sanctuary; and the end thereof shall be with a flood, and unto the end of the war desolations are determined.

27And he shall confirm the covenant with many for one week: and in the midst of the week he shall cause the sacrifice and the oblation to cease, and for the overspreading of abominations he shall make it desolate, even until the consummation, and that determined shall be poured upon the desolate.

First, a week in Hebraic terms can be defined as either a week of days or a week of years. Here, the context is years. Daniel is told that seventy weeks or seventy sevens of years (490) years are determined on "thy people and upon the holy city." Daniel was a Jew so the prophecy directly concerned the Jewish people and the city of Jerusalem. "After threescore and two weeks shall the Messiah be cut off" was a direct reference to Christ's death on the cross which was literally fulfilled with stunning accuracy. "The people of the prince that shall come shall destroy the city and the sanctuary" was also literally fulfilled when the Romans silenced the Jewish rebellion and destroyed the second Jewish temple stone by stone in 70 A.D. Jesus also prophesied that this event would take place years before it happened. Since the "people of the prince that shall come" were Romans, then it unveils the true identity of the coming Antichrist as a ruler over a modern day Roman Empire.

It is at the end of this pivotal prophecy, however, that the angel reveals to Daniel of how this particular Antichrist prince will "confirm the covenant with many for one week" or one seven year duration. History dictates that this final seven years out of the total 490 years determined upon the Jews is yet to be fulfilled because Jesus made it clear that He will return with great power and glory, *where every eye will see Him,* immediately after the great tribulation—that short time span located in the last half of this seven year period. Since He didn't return in this fashion seven years after His death, then it's more than solid proof that we are indeed in a holding pattern at this present moment which has now been going on for almost 2000 years and is settled right between the sixty-ninth and seventieth week of Daniel's prophecy. Of course, to add to the confusion, there are those who completely spiritualize Christ's Second Coming. They claim that it's not meant to be interpreted literally. It must be considered, however, that if He fulfilled the prophecies concerning His first appearance by physically coming to earth, then there's no reason to assume He wouldn't literally fulfill the prophecies concerning the Second Coming in the exact same manner!

This halt in the progression of Daniel's prophecy was the "mystery of God" Paul wrote about in Ephesians chapter 3. Again, it's a time period specifically designed to incorporate all nations into receiving the blessings of Abraham and also to provoke the nation of Israel to jealously with the intent of bringing them back to the truth. Since those of pre-tribulation *rapture* persuasion identify the genesis of this church era with the cessation of the sixth-ninth week in Daniel's prophecy, it is propagated that the church must be taken out before the last "week" can unfold because the last week is strictly specified for the Jews and designed solely for God's interaction with the land of Israel—not with the present day church. While it is true that the prophecy for Daniel's seventieth week is specifically addressed to the Jewish people, will the church actually be dismissed from this pivotal time period or will we see it? Does the Bible teach this current dispensation of grace to be a separation or integration concerning the last seven years before Christ's Second Coming?

Fortunately, the apostle Paul was specific enough and taught *integration of* the church period—not into the physical nation of Israel—but *into Daniel's seventieth week.* This is evident by how he addresses the church located in Rome where he gets a little more in depth about this current church age dispensation by using the analogy of an olive tree to help them (and us) understand the mysteries of this era with better clarification.

Romans 11:17
And if some of the branches be broken off, and thou, being a wild olive tree, wert grafted in among them, and with them partakest of the root and fatness of the olive tree;

The olive tree is representative of the promises made to Abraham which, currently, is manifested in this age as the gospel of Jesus Christ. The natural branches, or unbelieving Jews, were broken off due to their rejection of the Messiah which provided an avenue for the Gentiles to be grafted in. As a Gentile, if we believe in the Son, we have already won because we have become an insider! Then he writes:

Romans 11:25
*For I would not, brethren, that ye should be igno-rant of this **mystery**.*

The "mystery" Paul is referring to is the grafting in of the branches from the wild olive tree into the natural one. Since Paul was addressing this letter to a church in Rome— predominately, a Gentile congregation of believers—then ultimately, the mystery is the grafting in of the Gentile be-lieving part of the church into the olive tree through faith in Christ, becoming full partakers of the covenant promises originally made to Abraham. Paul concluded the verse with this:

that blindness in part is happened to Israel, until the fullness of the Gentiles be come in.

This statement is essential because it tells us what this current dispensation of God—the church age—is actually based upon. Even though a remnant of Jews accepted Chr-ist as the true Messiah during His ministry, Israel, *as a na-tion,* stepped into blindness because of their rejection. According to Romans 11:25, the blindness of unbelieving Israel is to continue until the fullness—or full number of Gentiles (allotted by God) has come into the church. The nation of Israel will <u>not</u> open its eyes until the very last Gentile has entered into the church and the church age doors have been closed.

This becomes an important piece to the equation be-cause, quite simply, to find out when this present church age and current dispensation of grace *ends* is to find out when Israel, *as a nation,* will finally step <u>out</u> of blindness. Since Christ is currently found to be the stumbling block and the root cause of their blindness, then the very simple yet critical truth of the matter is this: *The church age will continue until Israel accepts Jesus Christ as a nation!* Fortunately, the Scriptures rest in absolute harmony with this approach by actually revealing this moment to us in the very next verse of Romans chapter 11.

Romans 11:26-27
26And so all Israel shall be saved: as it is written, There shall come out of Sion the Deliverer, and shall turn away ungodliness from Jacob:
27For this is my covenant unto them, when I shall take away their sins.

Since Israel is still stooped in ungodly practices to date and will continue to be so throughout the great tribulation period, then these verses are speaking about the Second Advent of Christ in glory, during which, He will claim His rightly position of authority, open the eyes of Israel to His power, and cleanse them of their sins forever. He is to be the Deliverer who descends from Heavenly Sion (Hebrews 12:22) to set free the tyranny imposed on Israel by Satan at that time, offering the Jews one last chance of submission to the truth concerning His right to the throne.

It is to be emphasized at this juncture that Paul makes absolutely no mention of a great tribulation period as part of the progression of end time events following the "fullness of the Gentiles." It is clear from the passage that he doesn't list the church age first, followed by a time of great tribulation, and *then* Israel's salvation. Instead, he associates the church's end with Israel's salvation and repentance which is to strictly occur at Christ's post-tribulation return. These two events actually sit side by side in Romans chapter 11! Since the great tribulation (the second half of Daniel's last week) occurs just prior to the Second Coming of Christ, then this proves it to be a time period integrated within the church age.

Some may argue that Israel will begin to open their eyes during Daniel's last week and the great tribulation period, but the Scriptures reveal to the contrary. While pockets of Jews in Israel will indeed find salvation in Christ prior to His Second Coming (the 144,000 for example), the true context being spoken of here is Israel's awakening as an *entire nation*. Israel's repentance period, as a nation, is clearly portrayed as a post-tribulation event which will occur suddenly and instantaneously at Christ's second arrival and not gradually throughout the last seven years. The book of Zechariah addresses the timeframe of Israel's national repentance period specifically.

Zechariah 12:10-11,14
*[10]And I will pour upon the house of David, and upon the inhabitants of Jerusalem, the spirit of grace and of supplications: and **they shall look upon me** whom they have pierced, and they shall **mourn for him**, as one mourneth for his only son, and shall be in bitterness for him, as one that is in bitterness for his firstborn.*
[11]In that day shall there be a great mourning in Jerusalem, as the mourning of Hadadrimmon in the valley of Megiddon.
*[14]**All the families that remain**, every family apart, and their wives apart.*

Zechariah 13:1
In that day there shall be a fountain opened to the
house of David and to the inhabitants of Jerusalem
for sin and for uncleanness.

The very simply truth is this: The only way they can "look upon" Him is if they can actually *see* Him! Christ will have to physically come back to the land to open the eyes of the unrepentant nation of Israel. Once they see Him coming from the heavens onto earth in all of His splendor, it is then—and *only* then—that they will mourn for Him as a nation in realization of their blindness. Then God, at that time, will graciously give them an opportunity to cleanse themselves of their sins and turn to Him. This particular advent of Jesus Christ is scheduled to occur immediately after the great tribulation and after Daniel's seventieth week. This is when blindness will forever cease in Israel. It is when the veil will be finally lifted and the light let in. Since Paul, in Romans 11, clearly associates the end of the church age with this particular return of Christ and, at the same time, Israel's repentance (and not with the beginning of Daniel's seventieth week), then the indications are that the church will remain until the physical Second Coming of Jesus Christ to the land of Israel after the great tribulation.

-More Evidence of Integration-

Integration of this current dispensation of grace within Daniel's seventieth week is further exposed by studying the book of Revelation which describes much of the last few years before Christ's Second Coming. It reveals in many areas of how the power of Christ's gospel is still very much prevalent during that time. However, this integration can only be fully understood by explaining the evident synchronicity between the dispensation of grace and the good news of the Gospel. Paul made it quite clear to the churches of his day that they were, in fact, the same thing. First, he describes this current church age from the perspective of grace:

Ephesians 3:2
*If ye have heard of the **dispensation of the grace** of God which is given me to you-ward...*

However, Paul also recognized this dispensation of grace as a dispensation of the gospel as well:

I Corinthians 9:17
*For if I do this thing willingly, I have a reward: but if against my will, a **dispensation of the gospel** is committed unto me.*

The truth is, this current dispensation of grace is *also* the dispensation of the gospel. That gospel is (and always will be) the death, burial, and resurrection of Jesus Christ from which, by the *grace* of God, we can now obtain salvation through faith.

Ephesians 2:8
*For by **grace are ye saved through faith**; and that not of yourselves: it is the gift of God:*

While many try to split hairs over gospel definitions, it is apparent from Scripture that the current dispensation of grace we now live in is also defined as a dispensation of the gospel, which, in itself, is defined as salvation by *grace* through faith in Jesus Christ—a free gift to mankind. The striking truth is, the two dispensations are not independent from each other, but are in fact, *interdependent*—both faltering if separated in any way. With this necessary understanding, an obvious example of this current dispensation of grace and the power of the gospel can be easily found operating within the book of Revelation and intertwined with the final week of Daniel.

Revelation 14:6
And I saw another angel fly in the midst of heaven,
*having the **everlasting gospel** to preach unto them*
that dwell on the earth, and to every nation, and kindred, and tongue, and people,

Let no one ever try to confuse you with another gospel! This particular gospel found in the book of Revelation is the *same gospel* Paul adhered to in his day and that the angel is still declaring even throughout Daniel's seventieth week. It is heralded as an everlasting gospel, unchangeable, and constant from its conception and is still *clearly active* during the last seven years. Logic dictates that if grace ends—so does the good news of the gospel because of their proven interdependency on one another. Therefore, if it was true that the dispensation of grace ends at the beginning of Daniel's seventieth week, then the declaration made by the angel in Revelation 14:6 should not be there, nor should the terms "faith in Jesus" (Revelation 14:12), or "testimony of Jesus" (Revelation 11:17) because, they too, are built upon the concept of grace. Again, taking into consideration that it's entirely impossible to experience God's salvation through Jesus Christ without His grace, how do the "tribulation saints" eventually become born-again believers during the great tribulation if grace had already been stripped from them in a supposed pretribulation *rapture?* The fact is, it's *absolutely impossible* to claim that the dispensation of grace ends at the beginning of

Daniel's seventieth week because the power of the gospel—built upon the grace of God—is still very much alive during the tribulation period. Multitudes will experience this saving grace all the way through to Christ's Second Coming!

Careful and objective thinking reveals the pre-tribulation stance concerning a halt on the progression of grace during the last seven years to be severely erroneous. The fact that the power of the gospel is still prevalent within Daniel's last week proves that this current dispensation of grace will not end abruptly but, instead, will flow seamlessly into the last seven years and run parallel to the prophecies that are to unfold for the Jewish people at that same time. However, as I am to shortly point out, it is important to understand that God will only view this last seven years as a continuation of grace that began in the upper room on the day of Pentecost and nothing else. Since the church is indeed tied to the dispensation of grace, then it is for the present day church to witness, firsthand, the last seven years of this age as well.

-Trampling Underfoot the Son of God-

Those who teach a church exemption from the last seven years also propagate a reversion, by God, back to the previous Mosaic Law dispensation throughout Daniel's seventieth week in order to solely deal with the Jewish people. This teaching is an absolute necessity in upholding the pre-tribulation *rapture* viewpoint because it provides them with what they deem as a clear dividing line between the current dispensation of grace we now live in and Daniel's last week. Without it, there would be no clear scriptural distinction between the present day church and the saints of the tribulation period, essentially deflating the pre-tribulation view significantly.

A discrepancy in this viewpoint becomes quite apparent by simply viewing this claim from the perspective of God Himself. This is accomplished by reviewing the book of Hebrews. There, the writer was extremely careful to explain to the Jewish-Christian sect of his day of how the new covenant—established by Jesus Christ's death, burial, and resurrection—had now overtaken the old Mosaic Law. While most will not argue this point, what is most often overlooked is another more important and inescapable point: God established this new blood covenant as an *everlasting* and unfailing covenant that, in His own eyes, began with Christ's death on the cross into forever more!

Hebrews 13:20
Now the God of peace, that brought again from the dead our Lord Jesus, that great shepherd of the sheep, through the blood of the ***everlasting covenant***,

The truth is; for God to actually revert to the old Mosaic Law in order to deal with the Jewish people in the last seven years would be to trample *all over* the work Christ performed on the cross at Calvary! The famous "it is finished" statement Christ uttered before commending up His Spirit on that fateful day would have needed to be replaced with: "It is finished until God deals with Israel again." This, of course, is absolutely absurd! The author of Hebrews writes:

Hebrews 10:14-18
14For by one offering he (Jesus) hath perfected for ever them that are sanctified.
15Whereof the Holy Ghost also is a witness to us: for after that he had said before,

¹⁶This is the covenant that I will make with them after those days, saith the Lord, I will put my laws into their hearts, and in their minds will I write them;
¹⁷And their sins and iniquities will I remember no more.
¹⁸Now where remission of these is, <u>there is no more offering for sin</u>.

To claim that God will return to the dispensation of the Law and to animal sacrifices throughout the last seven years of this age is not only bold, it is ignorantly blasphemous. The book of Hebrews clearly states that God has set up a new *everlasting* covenant through the work of Jesus Christ on the cross, and that there are now no more continual offerings for sin other than the blood of Christ, nor will there ever be.

The definition of the word "dispensation" in the Webster dictionary is this: *A system of revealed commands and promises regulating human affairs.* God set the new promises on the shoulders of Jesus Christ 2000 years ago which now regulates the affairs of humans and disannuls animal sacrifices *forever more.* When He died on the cross, a new everlasting covenant was established, and not even the activities of the Jews within Daniel's seventieth week can annul it. While it is possible that the Jews could return to ritualistic animal sacrifices in the future, God will not (and cannot) honor these acts in any way, shape, or form. This is validated in Romans 11:26-27:

*²⁶And so all Israel shall be saved: as it is written, There shall come out of Sion the Deliverer, **and shall turn away ungodliness from Jacob***:
²⁷For this is my covenant unto them, when I shall take away their sins.

God's redemptive process for the nation of Israel begins with *Jesus Christ's post-tribulation Second Coming.* His agenda for them in the seventieth week is *not* to re-establish animal sacrifices, nor is it to revert to the heavy burdens associated with the Mosaic Law, but it is, quite simply, to back the nation of Israel into an inescapable corner during the last seven years so that they have absolutely no other alternative other than to recognize Jesus Christ as the chosen Messiah of Jehovah at His physical Second Coming. It is to get them with the *already-established program* set upon the foundations of Christ Jesus—to open their eyes to the current and everlasting covenant designed for both the physical and spiritual seed of Abraham. This frightening yet tactical agenda will simultaneously run its course side by side with the agenda that God has already established concerning salvation through Christ *throughout* Daniel's seventieth week, where He will continually point Israel toward the new everlasting covenant in Jesus Christ with exponentially increasing pressure. That pressure will become too much to bear for the tiny little nation when it is finally surrounded by Satan's enormous armies in the valley of Megiddo and will cry out to God to save them. God will answer this call by sending their long sought after Messiah—Jesus Christ—who will return with power and great glory and with an innumerable and unimaginable army. This is when Israel will finally and readily receive Christ as a whole nation, and their blindness will immediately cease at that moment. Until then, Scripture teaches that the nation of Israel will remain separate from the church and hidden from the promise made to Abraham until that great day of the Lord.

A Biblical Census of the Millennial Kingdom

After God has poured out His fury at the battle of Armageddon, a physical heavenly kingdom will be set up here on earth. This coming kingdom will be a time of true peace. Jesus Christ will sit on the throne in the line of David and rule the earth with a rod of iron from the city of Jerusalem. This kingdom will begin with His return to earth and will last for 1000 years. During that time, the earth will come under new regulations. The animal kingdom will behave in new, gentler ways, and the human life span will increase. The sun will be destroyed, and God's supreme glory will provide a perpetual light from then on. As a result, night will forever cease to exist. Human suffering will also be no more because God will wipe away all of our tears and all of our sorrow!

While many think the goal is to get to heaven, many have forgotten that it's actually heaven's goal to come to earth! Humanity has entered into such turmoil that if God didn't eventually intervene, we would ultimately destroy ourselves and the environment completely. Needless to say, we are destructive creatures, and it speaks volumes about our true sin nature and how we desperately need the Savior.

Questions have been raised about who will actually physically enter into this coming kingdom. Some like to make the case that if the church is actually *raptured* after the great tribulation and the wicked on the earth are destroyed, who would be left to populate the millennial kingdom of Christ? It's certainly an intriguing question, but a quick study of the Bible answers it.

First, consider the following: Even if you hold to a secret *rapture* 3 ½ - 7 years prior to the millennial reign, and the surviving tribulation saints are the ones to repopulate the earth, you still have the same problem to deal with! The Bible lists a resurrection to take place after the great tribulation—known as the first resurrection. Who does it involve?

> *Revelation 20:4-5*
> *⁴And I saw thrones, and they sat upon them, and judgment was given unto them: and I saw the souls of them that were **beheaded for the witness of Jesus, and for the word of God, and which had not worshipped the beast, neither his image, neither had received his mark upon their foreheads, or in their hands;** and they lived and reigned with Christ a thousand years.*
> *⁵**This is the first resurrection.***

This particular resurrection will involve all those with a testimony of Jesus and the Word of God, who did not worship the Beast or his image, nor receive his mark in their foreheads or in their hands. We know, without doubt, that this particular group of saints is to be persecuted *during* the great tribulation. Therefore, according to Revelation 20, those who are resurrected at the post-tribulation return of Christ (among others) are the *great tribulation saints*.

Then the argument becomes that only a resurrection takes place here and not the *rapture*. Unfortunately, many forget about Matthew 24:41—the parallel passage to the first resurrection of Revelation 20. This passage describes the post-tribulation *rapture* of those who are still alive and remain after the resurrection of the dead takes place.

> *Matthew 24:41.*
> *Two women shall be grinding at the mill; the* **one**
> **shall be taken**, *and the other left.*

These people aren't dead! They are involved in activities that only someone who is breathing oxygen can partake in! Again, to interpret this verse as the post-tribulation *rapture* of the living believers is by far the most harmonious confirmation of both *rapture* passages found in I Corinthians 15 and I Thessalonians 4 because we are told in each of those passages that both a resurrection of the dead <u>and</u> a *rapture* of the living are to occur together under one unified event. Staying within those guidelines, Revelation 20 supplies the description of the post-tribulation resurrection of the dead, while Matthew 24:41 parallels and describes the post-tribulation *rapture* of the living. Since the *rapture* is indeed padlocked to the first resurrection that occurs after the great tribulation, then those tribulation saints who are alive and remain will, they themselves, be caught up into the air after the dead have risen from their graves. If all the tribulation saints are resurrected and *raptured* at that time, they will be unable to populate the millennial kingdom because of their newly inhabited glorified bodies.

-The Fate of the Wicked-

Once the Messiah has collected His true church after the great tribulation, His attention will immediately be directed toward those gathered around the city of Jerusalem in the valley of Megiddo. This gathering will be the pinnacle of Satan's ultimate goal for Jewish genocide as he masses his troops around Israel's border in preparation for complete annihilation. Unfortunately for them, they will come face to face with a vengeful God. We learn in various passages throughout Scripture that the wicked are ultimately destroyed at this battle.

Zechariah 14:2
For I will gather all nations against Jerusalem to battle; and the city shall be taken, and the houses rifled, and the women ravished; and half of the city shall go forth into captivity, and the residue of the people shall not be cut off from the city.

Zechariah 12:9
And it shall come to pass in that day, that I will seek to destroy all the nations that come against Jerusalem.

Revelation 19:19
And I saw the beast, and the kings of the earth, and their armies, gathered together to make war against him that sat on the horse, and against his army.

Zechariah 14:5
...and the LORD my God shall come, and all the saints with thee.

Zechariah 12:4,13
4In that day, saith the LORD, I will smite every horse with astonishment, and his rider with madness: and I will open mine eyes upon the house of Judah, and will smite every horse of the people with blindness
13And it shall come to pass in that day, that a great tumult from the LORD shall be among them; and they shall lay hold everyone on the hand of his neighbour, and his hand shall rise up against the hand of his neighbour.

Revelation 20:19, 21
19And the beast was taken, and with him the false prophet that wrought miracles before him, with which he deceived them that had received the mark of the beast, and them that worshipped his image. These both were cast alive into a lake of fire burning with brimstone.
21And the remnant were slain with the sword of him that sat upon the horse, which sword proceeded out of his mouth: and all the fowls were filled with their flesh.

These passages speak loud and clear: After the church is caught up, the wicked gathered against Jerusalem in that day are destroyed. If the saints of the tribulation period (the church) are resurrected and *raptured* at Christ's Second Coming, and the wicked are destroyed at the battle of Armageddon, but the Bible still indicates a group of people living physically throughout the millennial reign, then who in the world is this mystery group, left to repopulate the millennial kingdom?

The short answer is, there will be a remnant of Jews and

Gentiles who will not partake in the *rapture* but will be saved from the ruthless day of the Lord and ushered into the millennial kingdom to be ruled by Christ and the resurrected and *raptured* saints. It is this remnant who will recognize Christ as the true Messiah strictly at His Second Coming and will immediately cry out and repent upon witnessing the resurrection and *rapture* of the saints.

Matthew 24:30
And then shall appear the **sign** *of the Son of man in heaven: and then shall all the tribes of the earth* **mourn**, *and they shall see the Son of man coming in the clouds of heaven with power and great glory.*

As explained in the first section of this book, the sign of the Son of man will be an unmistakable and unmatchable light; its source will be coming from the glory of Christ as He descends from heaven onto earth. **see page 22.* This sign will also incorporate the *rapture* of the church at that same time, only adding to the brilliance of light that will protrude the darkness of that day as we follow behind our victorious Messiah. Zechariah speaks of this spectacular transformation of the church in greater detail:

Zechariah 9:16
And the LORD their God shall save them **in that day** *(the day of the Lord) as the flock of his people: for they shall be as the stones of a crown, lifted up as an* **ensign** *upon his land.*

Stones of a crown are glorious in appearance and omit light that make them shine brilliantly. This is an excellent description of the glorious transformation that will occur at the resurrection and *rapture* of the church as she is being lifted up in the air, donning her glorified attire as an additional sign to those on the earth. The entire world, including a now-horrified army at Megiddo, will witness this blinding and frightening event and immediately recognize that they have been wrong about Jesus Christ and the message of believers all along. As a result, they will begin to cry out in anguish in realization of their mistake. As I have already mentioned in the previous chapter, a remnant of Jews will witness this spectacle from Israel and will join the world in mournful anguish.

Zechariah 12:10-14
*¹⁰And I will pour upon the house of David, and upon the inhabitants of Jerusalem, the spirit of grace and of supplications: and **they shall look upon me** whom they have pierced, and **they shall mourn for him**, as one mourneth for his only son, and shall be in bitterness for him, as one that is in bitterness for his firstborn*
*¹¹**In that day shall there be a great mourning** in Jerusalem, as the mourning of Hadadrimmon in the valley of Megiddon.*
*¹²**And the land shall mourn**, every family apart; the family of the house of David apart, and their wives apart; the family of the house of Nathan apart, and their wives apart;*
¹³The family of the house of Levi apart, and their wives apart; the family of Shimei apart, and their wives apart;
*¹⁴**All the families that remain**, every family apart, and their wives apart.*

Again, the only way they can look upon Him (Jesus) is if they can actually *see Him!* Once they witness the physical form of the true Messiah split the eastern skies and descend with His vast multitude of angels and saints in all of their glory, while simultaneously witnessing the ascension of the church rising from the earth to meet Him in the air, it is then that they will immediately mourn for Him because they will *finally* realize they have been wrong all along about the true Lordship of Jesus Christ. It is then that they will finally see Jesus as their true Messiah and realize that He is the one they have been so desperately waiting for.

This national mourning is important from a scholarly aspect because it is undeniable proof that they *did not partake in the rapture event* because, as you know, the *rapture* will be a time of great joy and not a time of sadness. Yet this wailing is still stated to take place in the land of Israel even after Christ's Second Coming. Since Zechariah's passage is set in a strict post-tribulation timeframe, it reveals that a remnant of Jews will indeed be left behind even after the post-tribulation *rapture* of the church. Fortunately, the story doesn't end there for them! Once the great battle of Armageddon has concluded, a time of repentance will immediately follow for all Jews who have survived these series of frightening events. This is addressed in the very next verse of Zechariah:

Zechariah 13:1
In that day there shall be a fountain opened to the house of David and to the inhabitants of Jerusalem for sin and for uncleanness.

It is this very group of Jews who are to survive the great tribulation and the battle of Armageddon on the great and terrible day of the Lord. It is also this particular group who will *physically enter* under the millennial rule of Jesus

Christ. Even the Lord Himself verifies this particular physical remnant of Israel to be present after the great day of the Lord.

Amos 9:8
Behold, the eyes of the Lord GOD are upon the sinful kingdom, and I will destroy it from off the face of the earth; (Satan/Antichrist's kingdom) **saving that I will not utterly destroy the house of Jacob**, *saith the LORD.*

Zechariah 13:8-9
⁸And it shall come to pass, that in all the land, saith the LORD, two parts therein shall be cut off and die; **but the third shall be left** *therein.*
⁹And I will bring the **third part** *through the fire, and will refine them as silver is refined, and will try them as gold is tried: they shall call on my name, and I will hear them: I will say, It is my people: and they shall say, The LORD is my God.*

Zephaniah 3:13
The **remnant of Israel** *shall not do iniquity, nor speak lies; neither shall a deceitful tongue be found in their mouth: for they shall feed and lie down, and* **none shall make them afraid.**

This overall succession of events, when interpreted in the correct order, begins to establish the true identity of the physical remnant found within the millennial age. First, Christ descends with power and great glory. Then, the church is *raptured* and the whole world, including the Jews within the borders of Israel, witnesses the event and mourns in despair over their monumental mistake. Christ goes on to defeat the enemies of Jerusalem at the battle of Armageddon, and a third of Israel physically remains in the aftermath. This physical Jewish remnant is then given a time for repentance and is finally ushered into the blessings of the millennial kingdom where they are ruled by Christ with a rod of iron for 1000 years. This information is tremendous in enlightening Romans 11:26 with even greater clarity:

Romans 11:26
*And so **all Israel shall be saved**:*

Again, the reason that all Israel will be saved is because any Jew who survives the great tribulation, witnesses the return of Christ, and *repents* will be spared. All others will be destroyed, leaving all of the remaining repentant Jewish remnant under Christ *as a nation*. The next verse in Romans verifies:

Romans 11:27
*...as it is written, There shall come out of Sion the Deliverer, and shall **turn away ungodliness from Jacob***

Jacob was the son of Abraham and was renamed by God.

Genesis 32:28
And he said, Thy name shall be called no more Jacob, but Israel: for as a prince hast thou power with God and with men, and hast prevailed.

Jacob is simply a symbolic name for the nation of Israel. When the Deliverer comes (Christ), He will turn all ungodliness away from the nation of Israel and so all Israel will be saved at that time.

-A Clue from Joel-

A more obscure indication of this short repentance period after the post-tribulation *rapture* can be found within the book of Joel. This evidence only begins, however, with the acknowledgement of the parallel found between Joel 2:11 and Paul's famous *rapture* passage of I Thessalonians.

Joel 2:11
*And the **LORD shall utter his voice** before his army: for his camp is very great: for he is strong that executeth his word: for the **day of the LORD** is great and very terrible; and who can abide it?*

As established in the first section of this book, this is a clear reference to the *rapture* of the church on the day of the Lord:

I Thessalonians 4:16, 5:2
*4:16For the **Lord himself shall descend from heaven with a shout***
*5:2For yourselves know perfectly that the **day of the Lord** so cometh as a thief in the night.*

Taking into consideration this evident parallel, it is what Joel writes in the next two verses that becomes of particular interest.

221

Joel 2:12-13
*12Therefore also **now**, saith the LORD, turn ye even
to me with all your heart, and with fasting, and with
weeping, and with **mourning**:*
*13And rend your heart, and not your garments, and
turn unto the LORD your God: for he is gracious and
merciful, slow to anger, and of great kindness, and
repenteth him of the evil.*

Please don't misunderstand; these few verses can certainly be applied to everyday living, but what must be understood is that the entire book of Joel strictly concerns the
future day of the Lord and the millennial reign. *It's strictly
prophetic in nature.* If adhering to the actual context of the
entire book, you will quickly realize that the "now" is to be
interpreted as a prophetic "now." Therefore, what is actually being relayed by the Lord Himself is that after He descends from heaven with a shout and gathers His saints at
the *rapture* of the church on the day of the Lord, even <u>now</u>
(at that point on the timeline) there will still be time to repent and turn back to Him. Need some convincing? Continue reading:

Joel 2:18
Then *will the LORD be jealous for his land, and pity
his people.*

What could be inserted here is: *Then*—after you have
witnessed the *rapture* and have turned your hearts back to
me—will the Lord be jealous for His land (Israel) and pity
His people. What will the Lord do at that point?

Joel 2:20
But I will remove far off from you the northern army, *and will drive him into a land barren and desolate, with his face toward the east sea, and his hinder part toward the utmost sea, and his stink shall come up, and his ill savour shall come up, because he hath done great things.*

Taking into consideration that the book of Daniel refers to the end time Antichrist as the "king of the north" in many areas of chapter 11, then this particular northern army is ultimately a reference to the *battle of Armageddon* which occurs at the end of our current age. This further proves the timeframe of this passage and adheres to the end time context so clearly evident throughout Joel's book. Considering this reference and paraphrasing the entire chapter, the actual message the Lord is conveying here is this: [After the *rapture* (which is to occur on the day of the Lord after the great tribulation), there will still be a small amount of time to repent and accept Me as your Savior. If you fully turn your hearts back to Me, I will then remove the armies surrounding Jerusalem at the battle of Armageddon.]

The Bible clearly indicates that the Jews will, in fact, cry out to Christ in this very manner as they witness His glorious re-entry into Jerusalem (Zech. 12). Christ will then honor His prophetic Word by defeating the armies at that battle of Armageddon and all Israel will be saved! The remaining Jews will then physically enter into the millennial kingdom under the strong authority of Jesus Christ.

-Gentile Remnant-

While the Jews will undoubtedly rejoice over their new found salvation and peace in the land of Israel, it is clear that this short post-tribulation repentance period—described in the book of Joel specifically from a Jewish perspective—will also incorporate Gentiles (non-Jewish) from around the world and is mentioned in other areas of Scripture, both in the Old and New Testament. Some of the most compelling evidence for physical Gentile citizenship within the millennial kingdom rests in Isaiah 59 and 60. To get a sense of the context and timeframe, a look at Isaiah 59 is needed first:

Isaiah 59:20
And the Redeemer shall come to Zion, and unto them that turn from transgression in Jacob, saith the LORD.

Again, this verse is a prophecy of Christ's Second Advent into the city of Jerusalem after the great tribulation and at the genesis of the millennial kingdom where the Jews are to turn to the true Messiah of Jehovah. Paul confirms this by specifically quoting it in Romans 11:26—clearly referencing Jesus Christ and His post-tribulation return to the land of Israel.

Romans 11:26
*And so all Israel shall be saved: as it is written, **There shall come out of Sion the Deliverer, and shall turn away ungodliness from Jacob**:*

This is the first proof of the context and timeframe in operation concerning Isaiah chapter 60. The second proof is found in Isaiah 60:1-2,11-19

¹Arise, shine; for thy light is come, and the glory of the LORD is risen upon thee. (Jerusalem)
²For, behold, the darkness shall cover the earth, and gross darkness the people: but the LORD shall arise upon thee, and his glory shall be seen upon thee.

Then down to verses 11 and 19...

Isaiah 60:11,19
¹¹Therefore thy gates shall be open continually; they shall not be shut day nor night; that men may bring unto thee the forces of the Gentiles, and that their kings may be brought.
¹⁹The sun shall be no more thy light by day; neither for brightness shall the moon give light unto thee: but the LORD shall be unto thee an everlasting light, and thy God thy glory.

While it could be that the gates of Jerusalem being described here are gates made by man, a parallel can be found at the end of the book of Revelation that confirms the true context and timeframe of Isaiah's passage once more.

Revelation 21:23-26
²³And the city had no need of the sun, neither of the moon, to shine in it: for the glory of God did lighten it, and the Lamb is the light thereof.
²⁴And the nations of them which are saved shall walk in the light of it: and the kings of the earth do bring their glory and honour into it.
²⁵And the gates of it shall not be shut at all by day: for there shall be no night there.
²⁶And they shall bring the glory and honour of the nations into it.

When studying this particular passage of Revelation, the discussion of the gates in verse 25 is actually in direct reference to the *heavenly* city of Jerusalem which will supernaturally descend onto earth after the 1000 year reign of Christ. Therefore, this parallel, combined with the citation made by the apostle Paul in Romans 11, proves that the timeframe of Isaiah 60 encapsulates the entire millennial reign which begins with Christ's Second Coming at the genesis of the millennial kingdom (Isaiah 59:20), and ends with the descent of heavenly Jerusalem onto earth after the millennial reign of Christ (Isaiah 60:11,19). These truths now give an allowance to boldly interpret the other verses found within Isaiah 60 from this confirmed millennial-era perspective.

Isaiah 60:3
And the **Gentiles shall come to thy light***, and kings to the brightness of thy rising.*

Although it doesn't initially identify the Gentiles mentioned here, it gives us the first indication of a group of Gentiles who are to actually survive the battle of Armageddon and enter the millennial kingdom. However, they aren't the only ones because verse 8 makes an incredible mention of the resurrected and *raptured* saints!

Isaiah 60:8
Who are these that fly as a cloud, and as the doves to their windows?

Isaiah is completely mystified by what he is seeing in his vision and can only ask himself: Who are these people flying around in the air like birds? Of course, what the prophet was actually witnessing was the highly anticipated resurrection and *rapture* of the church! Apparently the saints are going to have an alternative to walking once they receive their glorified bodies!

Additionally, this small mention of flying souls provides great Old Testament verification that the eagles of Matthew 24 are indeed to be allegorically attributed to the elect because the proven post-tribulation timeframe of Isaiah's passage is an identical match to that of Matthew 24—where Christ also *metaphorically* described a gathering of birds to be present at that time—the elect!

More importantly, from the perspective of this chapter, verse 8 makes a clear distinction between the *raptured* church and the Gentiles who come to the saving light that is to be projected from Christ's throne of glory in the earth-dwelling heavenly Jerusalem at that time. This distinction ultimately reveals that the Gentiles, depicted in verse 3, did not partake in the *rapture* event yet are still breathing air after the battle of Armageddon. Who is this mysterious Gentile group worthy enough to enter Christ's kingdom in their earthly bodies? Verse 14 fills us in:

Isaiah 60:14
The sons also of them that afflicted thee shall come bending unto thee; and all they that despised thee shall bow themselves down at the soles of thy feet; and they shall call thee; The city of the LORD, The Zion of the Holy One of Israel.

This is a powerful verse because it specifically identifies the Gentiles found to be physically dwelling within the millennial kingdom. It would have been a Gentile group who would have previously <u>despised</u> the earthly city of Jerusalem and what it represented prior to Christ's Second Advent. *This makes it impossible to associate this particular group of Gentiles with the tribulation saints because the tribulation saints would have never despised Jerusalem at anytime.* Any genuine follower of Christ, whether now or during the great tribulation, understands the significance of this Holy City and the pivotal role it plays concerning their faith. To say you love Christ yet hold contempt for the city of Jerusalem and its people would be contrary. This will not be a view held by the tribulation saints.

Therefore, even if you believe that the tribulation saints are separate from the present day church, and that they are the ones to physically enter the millennial kingdom, the book of Isaiah still clearly indicates an additional group of Gentiles to be present in that kingdom. This Gentile group would have despised Jerusalem throughout the great tribulation period until Christ's Second Coming where they would have finally joined the Jews in wailing over the realization of their monumental mistake concerning Jesus. Of course, I must reiterate at this point that it is entirely impossible for the tribulation saints to physically enter under the 1000 year rule of Christ because it has already been well-established that they are to be resurrected (Revelation 20:4) and *raptured* (Matthew 24:40-41), and in relation to Isaiah 60, are to be categorized with Isaiah's vision of floating souls in verse 8.

Dissecting Isaiah 60:14 further, another reference is made to the "sons also of them." To find out who the "sons also of them" are is to figure out who "they" are. "They" are those who will be gathered against the Jews in Israel at the future battle of Armageddon. "They" will be the *wicked Gentiles* in total subjection to the Antichrist and will be gathered with many armies in the "valley of decision" around Jerusalem. "They" will be utterly destroyed by Christ at His Second Coming. Therefore, the "sons of them" are speaking of the Gentile remnant left from all of the nations who will eventually gather around Jerusalem and be crushed at the battle of Armageddon on the day of the Lord. This surviving Gentile remnant would have not been a part of the church (tribulation saints) throughout the great tribulation period. But like the church, they would have also chosen not to worship the Antichrist figure or take the Beast's mark (for their own personal reasons), neither would they have been found subject to the armies gathered at the battle of Armageddon at the end, but like the Jews in the land of Israel, will also be given a very small window of opportunity to submit to the new authority of Jesus Christ in the Holy City once the great battle has concluded.

Zechariah also specifically addresses this Gentile remnant to be present in the millennial age which begins with a description of Christ's return from heaven:

Zechariah 14:4
And his feet shall stand in that day upon the mount of Olives, which is before Jerusalem on the east, and the mount of Olives shall cleave in the midst thereof toward the east and toward the west, and there shall be a very great valley; and half of the mountain shall remove toward the north, and half of it toward the south.

Here, He will call for the repentant remnant worthy enough to enter into His kingdom:

Joel 2:32
*And it shall come to pass, that **whosoever shall call on the name of the LORD shall be delivered:** for in mount Zion and in Jerusalem shall be deliverance, as the LORD hath said, and **in the remnant whom the LORD shall call.***

And back to Zechariah:

Zechariah 14:16
*And it shall come to pass, that **every one that is** **left** of all the nations which came against Jerusalem shall even go up from year to year to worship the King, the LORD of hosts, and to keep the feast of tabernacles.*

Those of the surviving Gentile remnant (from the nations that came against Jerusalem to ultimately war against Jesus Christ) who have denied the mark of the Beast, witness the Second Coming of Christ, answer the call of Jesus from the city of Jerusalem, and immediately turn their hearts to the Lord will enter the kingdom in their physical bodies alongside the saved Jewish people, and all—including the resurrected/*raptured* saints and angels of heaven—will worship Him year after year.

Troubled by Tribulation

My prayer is that, by this point, God has illuminated the truth of His Word to you. The true church will indeed go through the great tribulation and endure severe persecution as a result. If you are still not convinced, but at anytime throughout these pages you've heard that tiny voice in the back of your head tell you: "Could there actually be some truth to all of this?" Don't ignore it! It's a gentle nudge in the right direction. God will lead you to the truth—*if you let Him*. If you ask Him to reveal it to you, He certainly will; I'm a living testament to that.

I have challenged people to seek God for clarity in this area in the past. I know that most of them never did (with any diligence anyway) because they are still blinded. God is certainly faithful. If you truly want clarity, He'll give it to you, but you must diligently seek Him. God rewards those who do just that. When you eventually find what you were asking for, you must humble yourself and accept the truth whether you agree with the reasoning behind it or not. If each did their part in this area, I would have never had to write this book in the first place, and the church would be a stronger-bonded entity and a spiritual force to be reckoned with.

Those who do finally come to the realization that the church will not be spared from the great tribulation generally experience an immediate wave of overcoming fear. Most at this point ask: Why?! Why would a loving God allow this to happen to His own people? Well...why did God allow Paul to be chased, whipped, beaten, persecuted, stoned, shipwrecked, and jailed? Why did He allow Stephen to die for his faith? Why did Antipas, from the church of Pergamos, die a martyr's death? Why was John banished to a small island for his testimony? Why did Christ prophecy over the apostle Peter that he would be led where he did not want to go—indicating that, he too, would suffer a martyr's death? Why were Christians mercilessly tortured, thrown to lions, burned at the stake, and used as street lamps in Rome? I could go on and on.

Today, when we think of the words persecution and tribulation, we think: "My co-worker makes fun of me because of my belief" or "They are constantly pressuring me into partaking in their ungodly practices." While that certainly is a part of it all, Biblically speaking, it actually encapsulates minor persecution all the way to a _martyr's death_. Keep that in mind the next time you encounter these terms in the Bible because every time they appear, they are actually speaking of a possible death for what you believe!

Really, if you truly consider it, how could anything that happened to the saints in the early church be any worse than what we are soon to endure in the great tribulation? The only separation stems from the fact that the great tribulation will be the largest, most concentrated and ruthless assault against believers (and Jews) that will ever occur in history; however, Satan's intention will remain the same as it was when the church was in its infancy: Eradication.

Many in the early church died for the faith. Although we don't hear much about it, many are dying a martyr's death today. An unfathomable amount of believers will die at the end yet here in America (and wherever else), we have become far too ignorant, comfortable, and complacent to even remember the truth of it all. For whatever reason, God has shielded us for a season; but in the meantime, the idea of this type of persecution has become completely foreign to us. I believe this to be why the pre-tribulation *rapture* theory is flourishing. It gets us off the hook. It doesn't make us accountable. It's fantastical. It's an easy pill to swallow, and it appeals to our selfishness. It certainly reflects our character the best. America is obsessed with instant gratification, and it fits in very nicely with our credit cards, microwaves, dishwashers, and drive-through windows.

Now consider the Chinese church. Today, they are under immense persecution and are experiencing most of the trials the early church had to face in its day. They laugh at the notion of a pre-tribulation *rapture!* With all the persecution that has preceded us and that which is still happening today within the church, what makes us think we are exempt? The truth is, *we are not!* Satan will continue to come against us, including a last grand-ditch effort at the end before his worldly kingdom is consumed by God.

So why all of this trouble in our lives? First, the tribulations we endure are an outward manifestation of our profession in Christ.

II Thessalonians 1:4-5
4So that we ourselves glory in you in the churches of God for your patience and faith in all your persecutions and tribulations that ye endure:

*5Which is a manifest token of the righteous judgment
of God, that ye may be counted worthy of the kingdom of God, for which ye also suffer:*

The suffering we endure for the sake of righteousness is
evidence that we are going in the right direction; it's outward evidence of adoption into the kingdom family. If you
are floating in a canoe down a river, then everything seems
trouble-free. You don't even have to paddle if you don't
want to. It's if you decide to turn around that the real work
begins. Suddenly, what seemed easy has now become difficult because you are going against the flow that surrounds
you. In today's world, if you go with the flow you will certainly be washed away. Turn around, pick up your paddle,
and dig in! That's the life of a true believer. You may want
to give up sometimes but remember, the Lord is in the
stern! He'll provide added strength so that you can endure
the turbulent waters. He'll steer you in the right direction!
Tribulation in our lives also gives God grounds to return
trouble upon your adversaries.

II Thessalonians 1:6
*Seeing it is a righteous thing with God to recom-
pense tribulation to them that trouble you;*

Our suffering seems to go unnoticed at times and for the
most part, it will—in this life. But God notices. The world
wants our demise; Satan wants our demise. We are peculiar
to them, and the light we project pierces through them like
an open book. While we choose to endure the sufferings at
the hands of Satan in his present worldly system, the
wicked are unknowingly storing up terrible judgments
upon themselves as they cruise down the easy street of today. They may not feel the effects in this present world, but

they will surely feel them in the one to come. Paul reminds us:

> *II Thessalonians 1:7-9*
> *7And to you who are troubled rest with us, when the Lord Jesus shall be revealed from heaven with his mighty angels,*
> *8In flaming fire taking **vengeance** on them that know not God, and that obey not the gospel of our Lord Jesus Christ:*
> *9Who shall be punished with everlasting destruction from the presence of the Lord, and from the glory of his power;*

We are reminded however:

> *Romans 12:19*
> *Dearly beloved, avenge not yourselves, but rather give place unto wrath: for it is written, Vengeance is mine; I will repay, saith the Lord.*

Leave it up to God. It's not up to us to seek revenge on those who persecute us. Vengeance belongs to the Lord alone, and is being stored up for that dreadful day of the Lord God Almighty. In relation, Paul writes:

> *Romans 12:20*
> *Therefore if thine enemy hunger, feed him; if he thirst, give him drink: for in so doing thou shalt heap coals of fire on his head.*

Ever heard the term: "kill 'em with kindness"? By blessing those who persecute you, you're essentially confirming a death sentence upon them. God will judge your enemies accordingly. He is a righteous judge; He will not issue out sentences unjustly. He will only punish the deserving. The deserving are all those who refuse the good news of Jesus Christ. He will, in His due time, avenge you upon your behalf. However, I would like to point out that our motives for loving our enemies should not be because we desire their total destruction, but that we want to win them for Christ. If we say we love God, then we should reflect His character. God loves everyone—that includes the lost and dying. He wants *all* to come to repentance so that none are destroyed. We should desire the same.

Another reason we are to endure persecution is because it shows God "who's who"

Philippians 1:28
And in nothing terrified by your adversaries: which is to them an evident token of perdition, but to you of salvation, and that of God.

It draws the proverbial line in the sand. Who will stand on God's side to serve Him and who will oppose Him? Those standing against God in the day of His return will suffer the consequences severely at the end of this age. In verse 29, the truth is finally laid out plain for the church:

Philippians 1:29
*For unto you it is given in the behalf of Christ, not only to believe on him, but also to **suffer for his sake**;*

The Word is its own best interpreter and, here in Philippians, it becomes undeniable that true believers are to suffer for the cause of Christ. It's given to us! To think that we are exempt is foolish and ignores the Scripture completely.

On a lower level, we are given everyday trials. Our profession of faith doesn't nullify that. In fact, that profession, if genuine, will produce them! There's too much off-balance prosperity preaching these days. Sugar-coating messages with the intent of increasing weekly church attendance does nothing but produce a bunch of loosely grounded believers and a wealthy preacher. When the first trial comes, they run because they didn't get what they were told they deserve. Well actually, they *did* get what they deserved—a doubled-minded faith and an empty hand! Don't misunderstand; I believe that God surely wants to overrun you with His blessings, but those blessings won't come unless *you're carrying your cross*. The path we choose is to live for Christ, in which, suffering for His sake will surely occur. Count on it! Believers need to be taught this from day one.

The wicked, on the other hand, have chosen their path whether they make a conscious decision about it or not. This draws a separation between those who love sin from those who love God. Christ's suggestion is that we seek His riches and not those of the world. The only way we are able to obtain them is through the fire of tribulation in our lives.

Revelation 3:18
I counsel thee to buy of me gold tried in the fire, that thou mayest be rich; and white raiment, that thou mayest be clothed, and that the shame of thy nakedness do not appear; and anoint thine eyes with eyesalve, that thou mayest see.

Why?

I Peter 1:7,9
7That the trial of your faith, being much more precious than of gold that perisheth, though it be tried

with fire, might be found unto praise and honor and glory at the appearing of Jesus Christ
⁹Receiving the end of your faith, even the salvation of your souls.

Trials refine us, to which, the end of our faith is salvation of our souls and eternal rest with Jesus Christ.

Trials also test and strengthen our character in Christ.

Romans 5:3-5
³And not only so, but we glory in tribulations also: knowing that tribulation worketh patience;
⁴And patience, experience; and experience, hope:
⁵And hope maketh not ashamed; because the love of God is shed abroad in our hearts by the Holy Ghost which is given unto us.

Another word for experience is proof. Once we come through the fire we know that because God delivered us from that particular affliction, we can surely place our hope in Him to get us through the next one. Romans 5:5 states: *hope maketh not ashamed,* which could be translated: Trusting in God will never fail or disappoint you.

The next time tribulation comes your way, know that God is there to see you through it all. I know that it's extremely hard to see the positive in a dire situation sometimes, but we must embrace tribulation knowing that if we continue in our faith, it will be used by Him to refine our flesh in some way and, in the end, we will come out of it more purified than before. I'm in the midst of my own trial even as I write these words, so I'm preaching to myself more than you; but nevertheless, it applies to all.

If we end up suffering the most severe persecution and lose our lives (and yes, the Bible teaches that such can be the case), remember; our reward is immense, beyond measure, and incomprehensible. Paul wrote:

II Corinthians 12:2-5
2I knew a man in Christ above fourteen years ago, (whether in the body, I cannot tell; or whether out of the body, I cannot tell: God knoweth;) such an one caught up to the third heaven.
3And I knew such a man, (whether in the body, or out of the body, I cannot tell: God knoweth;)
4How that he was caught up into paradise, and heard unspeakable words, which it is not lawful for a man to utter.
5Of such an one will I glory: yet of myself I will not glory, but in mine infirmities.

And:

Philippians 1:21
For to me to live is Christ, and to die is gain.

Even though our enemies may seem to have the upper hand right now, know that one day very soon, God will judge them for their wickedness on that great day of His return.

Conclusion

Please understand that I am not here to attack you personally if you choose to believe in variances. *It's false doctrine that I war against.* While the Bible is clear on its position, the choice is still your own. You can either accept it or reject it. Ultimately, it is up to you whether you veer left or right on this issue. You can speculate here and assume there, or you can be ready to face the facts even if it includes accepting the dire implications.

If I still haven't convinced you of the information presented in this book, then this next sentence may be the most offensive one you will read, but I believe courage must be mustered and the truth be told: *The pre-tribulation rapture theory is devils' doctrine to its very core.* While most authors opposed to the pre-tribulation *rapture* theory will dance around this fact, the days of walking on eggshells must come to an end. Its total opposition to literal interpretation and parallelism (that only the most savvy of Bible Scholars can attempt in explaining away), and its complete disregard for sound contextual interpretation leaves an easily identifiable Satanic mark out in the open for all to see.

Undoubtedly, this makes you angry that I would be so arrogant to slap such a label on something you believe is adamantly taught in the Bible, but I urge you to put down your pride because it is pride that will keep you from the truth! We must *all* revisit the Word of God with child-like earnestness. I am sounding all alarms within the church. <u>Now is the time to wake up!</u> The Bible teaches that, at the time of the end, people will fall victim to various devils' doctrine. *This is surely one of them* and it is ramped among the church today. Satan is certainly using this subtle divide and conquer tactic to flank God's people at the right time. It is a major setup for downfall and is a virus that can only be snuffed out by understanding God's Word as a body of believers.

I would like to make it clear, however, that not everyone teaching this doctrine from the pulpit are all ministers of Satan. I believe that ninety-nine percent of today's preachers are simply unaware that during their years in seminary, they were being spoon-fed only one aspect of eschatological doctrine from a biased perspective. Even though other viewpoints may have been lightly covered, they graduated without a clear understanding of any other position. I can attest to this very fact from personal experience because there are people in my life who are Bible college graduates, who also claim they were shown both sides of the coin. Yet when I began to show them even some of the very basics of the post-tribulation position, they admitted that it was the first time they had ever heard it described in that way. This is because any college professor who personally advocates a pre-tribulation *rapture* can never really represent the post-tribulation *rapture* view adequately enough because the building blocks of both positions are fundamentally opposite. A critical mistake is made when attempting to carry the building blocks of the pre-tribulation theory over to try to establish the post-tribulation position—which will never work; it's a major reason why the post-tribulation position is deemed to be flawed. To accurately teach the post-tribulation position, the slate must be *completely* wiped clean, and an entirely different set of building blocks must be used right from the very beginning—building blocks that most pre-tribulation proponents don't possess. Unfortunately, in the end, no one is given a fair opportunity to make a well-informed decision. Would the church be inundated with the pre-tribulation theory as much as it is now if up-and-coming pastors were also given a clear and unbiased case for the post-tribulation viewpoint? I believe the pre-tribulation *rapture* theory would be eradicated—and quickly.

Some think that this overall issue is not-at-all important, that we are not to quarrel in the church over trivial things, and that the salvation of lost souls is priority number one. I absolutely agree. Reaching the lost *is* number-one priority; but once they enter into the fold, shouldn't they be given the truth in *all* areas and given the right tools to succeed? Tailoring an escapist mindset is extremely dangerous; the Bible is clear: He who endures *to the end* will be saved, and all those who take the mark of the Beast will be separated and destroyed by God Almighty—a very dark thought indeed.

Be honest with yourself for a minute; if you knew there was a possibility that you might actually have to endure the great tribulation, wouldn't you rethink your walk with God on all levels? How much faith do I really have? Is my prayer life the way it should be? Are there things in my life that are hindering my relationship with Him? Do I trust Him fully? Will I be able to lean on Him 100% in extremely dire circumstances? And the big question is this: *Am I really willing to die for my faith?* These were all valid questions to be asking yourself if you were part of the first century church and they weren't even in the great tribulation yet! You have to admit, these questions become increasingly important when faced with the real possibility of persecution. To me it seems vital—especially with the times we are living in—that we strengthen our battle armor now while there is still a small amount of time left.

Would you want to enter a war that started out with a surprise attack and left you dazed with ratty weapons and protection? Imagine for a moment, to your total dismay, that you find the mark has been implemented as mandatory with the penalty of torture and death if you do not comply. Imagine the confusion that might war in your mind at that point. *"Where is our Savior? I thought we weren't going to have to endure this? Why would He allow this? Did He turn His back on me? I thought He loved me? Am I even saved? Everyone told me we'd be gone by now—what is going on? I am not prepared for this! Maybe I should just submit to this world system; otherwise, how am I supposed to live? God didn't come to save us like He promised so maybe the Bible is a bunch of bologna anyway!"* Do you see the potential war that could take place in your own mind if one was not prepared in advance? This is the desired result of the enemy and *the road for all those who have placed their unwavering trust in a rapture of the church prior to the great tribulation.* It's Satan's full intent to set you up for failure so that, in the last few years, he can whisper to you to submit to his authority in the midst of this ongoing battle for your mind.

Know also, that at the same time, it will be an *all out satanic war* waged against Israel and the church for your physical death if you do not comply—just as it was in the days of the early church. Fortunately, as of right now, we face limited battles from the enemy. We must win our battles now if we are to successfully overcome him spiritually in the final war.

Church, it is time to rise up, link arms, and prepare ourselves as a united warrior against the evil of those days.

A Special Word for Pre-tribulation Rapture Pastors and Teachers

Scriptures reveal that those who teach the Word of God to others are held to a higher accountability. Where much is given, much is required. The rewards will surely be grand, but the repercussions will match if the people are led away from *any* part of God's truth. With that kind of responsibility resting upon you, I respectfully ask: Are you *really willing* to bank all of your money on nothing more than a theory (I emphasize the word theory), then hope for the best when you stand before God? Honestly, do you *really* want to be outside of the truth on this issue? Unless you're a willful false prophet, then I know the answer is an emphatic no.

Unfortunately, the pre-tribulation *rapture* theory is being taught everywhere these days like it's set in concrete, poured out from heaven onto the pages of the Bible. Have you ever considered that you might actually be in error? Again, have you really considered it? I'm not being condescending, nor am I trying to bully you; I'm simply trying to put it all in fresh perspective. You must fully understand the ramifications. On that great Day of Judgment, even though you will be saved, any works performed in this life that were not originally prepared by God for you to do will be immediately burned up, ultimately eating away at what could have been a much larger eternal reward. I'm begging you with every fiber of my being—ask <u>God</u> to directly reveal this entire matter to you. Seek Him daily on this issue. He will reveal the truth to you so long as you seek Him diligently, and with an open and humble heart. It's that simple. I'm metaphorically jumping up and down right now, waving my arms trying to get your attention because this is going to become of the utmost importance much sooner than you think.

This book is not essential to opening your eyes. Seeking Godly wisdom is. I'm simply trying to coax you into a position of earnest prayer on this matter. If you do, then my job is done because I am 100% certain that you will ascertain the truth. Perhaps your initial intention is to seek God to prove me wrong. That's fine, but please don't go into your prayer closet with closed-mindedness. Be ready to accept whatever God shows you whether you agree with it or not because there's absolutely no time to stall now. This kind of humbleness will only come with preparation however. Prepare yourself first, or you are wasting your time and God's.

Unfortunately, we've come to a point where there's barely any time left and many souls hang in the balance. You know and I know that we are in the last-of-the-last days before Christ returns. Daniel's seventieth week could literally begin <u>*tomorrow*</u>. Please don't brush it off like it's highly unlikely that you will be the one standing behind a pulpit or in front of a classroom when the last seven years begin to unfold before your eyes. *Many prophetic signs point to the fact that it could very well be you!*

I can only imagine what kind of church service that poor lonely Pastor will probably have the following Sunday (before it's outlawed) when his congregation realizes they aren't going anywhere. He's sure to have an angry mob on his hands screaming: "Why didn't you tell us?!" That's a big gamble if you ask me! A lot of muddled explanations will have to be dished out quickly and trust will be lost in one single instant. Ah...division—Satan's trademark!

In these end-of-the-end times, you must make *all* efforts to expound the truth—not only to protect the people, but yourself as well. *To stand up and speak the truth in <u>all areas of doctrine</u> in these last days is paramount.*

I won't lie to you; it will probably cost you. You might lose fair-weather believers. You might even lose an entire congregation, but I know the God I serve will always honor you if you make the right choices. Friend, serve God—even if it involves a hot-button issue such as this one. To prepare the ones who will listen now is absolutely critical. As painful as it may be, if others can't handle the truth and walk out, simply allow the Holy Spirit to work in their lives. Unfortunately, the church is rapidly approaching a serious weeding, and this will be a part of it all—mark these very words. Don't get left by the wayside. God bless you in your endeavors.

If this book was purchased at Amazon.com and production quality is found to be unsatisfactory, please contact them immediately to ensure a new book is sent.

Please visit the official *Changed©* website at:
www.theposttribulationrapture.com